MW01120549

10 Minute Guide to
The Norton Utilities® 6

Paul McFedries

A Division of Macmillan Computer Publishing
11711 North College, Carmel, Indiana 46032 USA

To my parents, without whom...

International Standard Book Number: 0-672-30183-0
Library of Congress Catalog Card Number: 91-66261

Publisher: *Richard K. Swadley*
Publishing Manager: *Marie Butler-Knight*
Managing Editor: *Marjorie Jo Hopper*
Acquisitions Editor: *Mary-Terese E. Cozzola Cagnina*
Development Editor: *Lisa Bucki*
Manuscript Editor: *Joe Kraynak*
Cover Design: *Dan Armstrong*
Book Design: *Scott Cook*
Indexer: *Sue VandeWalle*
Production: *Jeff Baker, Scott Boucher, Brad Chinn, Brook Farling, Sarah Leatherman, Juli Pavey, Howard Peirce, Joe Ramon, Mae Louise Shinault, Bruce Steed*
Special thanks to *Gregg Bushyeager* for ensuring the technical accuracy of this book.

Printed in the United States of America

ii

Trademarks

All terms mentioned in this book that are known to be trademarks or service marks are listed below. In addition, terms suspected of being trademarks or service marks have been appropriately capitalized. SAMS cannot attest to the accuracy of this information. Use of a term in this book should not be regarded as affecting the validity of any trademark or service mark.

dBASE is a registered trademark of Ashton-Tate Corporation.

Lotus, Symphony, and 1-2-3 are registered trademarks of Lotus Development Corporation.

PostScript is a registered trademark of Adobe Systems Incorporated.

The Norton Utilities and UnErase are registered trademarks and Norton Disk Doctor, Speed Disk, Calibrate, and Symantec are trademarks of Symantec Corporation.

WordStar is a registered trademark of MicroPro International Corporation.

Contents

Introduction

From time to time, all computer users suffer from the frustrations of inadvertently deleted files, accidental disk formats, and damaged data. But now that you have The Norton Utilities, you'll be able to do something about it. The Norton Utilities is a collection of programs designed to help you recover from these problems and to make DOS more manageable.

Now What?

You could wade through the four or five manuals that came with the program to find out how to perform a specific task, but that may take a while and it may tell you more than you want to know. You need a practical guide, one that will tell you exactly how to perform a given task.

Welcome to the 10 Minute Guide to The Norton Utilities 6

Because most people don't have the luxury of sitting down uninterrupted for hours at a time to learn The Norton Utilities, this *10 Minute Guide* does not attempt to teach *everything* about the program. Instead, it focuses on the most often-used features. Each feature is covered in a single self-contained lesson, which is designed to take 10 minutes or less to complete. And because each lesson is self-contained, you can turn to any lesson at any time to learn how to perform a specific task.

The *10 Minute Guide* teaches you about the program without relying on technical jargon. With straightforward, easy-to-follow explanations and numbered lists that tell you what keys to press and what options to select, the *10 Minute Guide to The Norton Utilities 6* makes learning the program quick and easy.

What Is The Norton Utilities?

The Norton Utilities is a collection of over two dozen programs designed to give you greater control over your computer by simplifying and extending DOS. With the Norton program, you can unerase accidentally deleted files, fix corrupted files, find files that have been misplaced on your hard drive.

Version 6.0 offers the following new features:

- Support for DOS 5.0's undelete, unformat, and LOADHI features.

- A new configuration utility, NUCONFIG, that enables you to reconfigure The Norton Utilities without having to reinstall the program.

- A new version of the Speed Disk program that has been improved so that it runs much faster than previous versions.

- Command line utilities such as File Save and Line Print, unavailable in Version 5, have been reinstated.

- Safe Format now supports the 2.88-megabyte floppy disk format.

How to Use This Book

The *10 Minute Guide to The Norton Utilities 6* consists of a series of lessons ranging from basic startup to a few more advanced features. Remember, however, that nothing in this book is difficult. Although most users will want to start at the beginning of the book and progress through the lessons sequentially, you can complete the lessons in any order. I do recommend, however, that you read at least Lessons 1 and 3 before skipping ahead. These two Lessons discuss using the main Norton menu and offer basic mouse and keyboard techniques you will need throughout the book.

If The Norton Utilities has not been installed on your computer, consult the inside front cover for installation steps. If you need to review basic DOS commands for preparing diskettes, see the "DOS Primer" at the end of this book.

Icons and Conventions Used in This Book

The following icons have been added throughout the book to help you find your way around:

Timesaver Tip icons offer shortcuts and hints for using the program efficiently.

Plain English icons define new terms.

Panic Button icons appear where new users often run into trouble.

The following conventions have been used to clarify the steps you must perform:

What you type or select The information you type or the options you select appear in second color.

On-screen text Any text that appears on screen is shown in a special type called monospace.

Menu names The names of menus, commands, buttons, and dialog boxes are shown with the first letter capitalized for easy recognition.

About the Screens

Screen reproductions in this book were created using *Collage Plus* from Inner Media, Inc., Hollis, NH.

Because I was using The Norton Utilities with a VGA monitor, I was able to take full advantage of Norton's graphical displays. If you have a CGA, EGA, or monochrome monitor, your screens may vary. For example, you may not see some of the icons; check boxes may appear as brackets [ ] instead of boxes; and radio buttons may appear as parentheses ( ) instead of circles.

For Further Reference...

To learn more about The Norton Utilities, look for this slightly more advanced book, also by Sams: *The First Book of The Norton Utilities 6*, by Joseph B. Wikert, revised by Lisa Bucki.

Lesson 1
Starting and Exiting the Norton Menu Program

In this lesson, you will learn how to start and exit the Norton menu program.

The Norton Menu Program

The Norton Utilities contains more than two dozen programs, each with its own rules and regulations. If you like, you can run each program individually from the DOS prompt as you would any program (see Lesson 2). Alternatively, you can use a program called Norton, which lists all the Norton utilities on a single, easy-to-use menu.

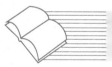

> **Utility Programs** The terms *program* and *utility* will be used interchangeably throughout this book.

Starting Norton

To start the Norton menu program

- At the DOS prompt, type **norton** and press Enter.

After a copyright message is displayed for a few seconds, the Norton menu appears (see Figure 1-1). Use this screen to start the other Norton utilities. The screen contains the following elements:

- The menu bar at the top of the screen contains the Norton pull-down menus (see Lesson 3, "Norton Utilities Basics," for information on accessing menus using the keyboard and mouse).

- The Commands window lists the Norton utilities.

- The Description window describes both the highlighted program and some of its most commonly used options.

- The Norton command line displays the command name associated with each program. For example, the command name for the Norton Disk Doctor utility is NDD.

If you are using Norton for the first time, the word **RECOVERY** is highlighted in the Commands window. This is one of four topics that Norton uses to group similar programs together (the other topics are Speed, Security, and Tools). This makes it easier to find the utility you want and reduces the complexity of The Norton Utilities by breaking the entire package down into smaller groups.

Running Utilities from the Norton Menu

The Norton menu provides you with easy access to all of the Norton utilities. To run a utility from the menu, follow these steps:

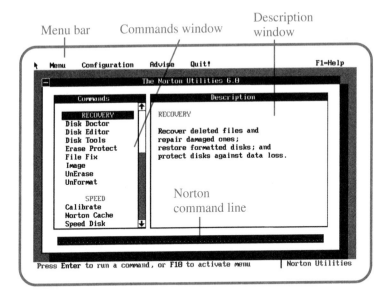

Menu bar   Commands window   Description window

Norton command line

Figure 1-1. The Norton main menu.

1. Press ↓ to move through the list of commands in the
   Commands window. Each command runs a different
   utility. Notice that the screen changes each time the
   highlight moves to a different command:

   • The Description window changes to display
     information about the highlighted command.
     When you highlight a command, you are shown
     the proper syntax for the command, a brief
     description of its function, and some commonly
     used switches. When you highlight a topic
     heading (for example, **RECOVERY**), you are
     given a general description of the types of
     programs included in the topic.

   • The Norton command line changes to display
     the command line name associated with the
     highlighted program.

3

Terminology Don't worry if you aren't familiar with terms such as "switches," "syntax," or "command line." New words and concepts are inevitable when you learn about a software package. To help you along, these and other terms will be explained throughout this book.

As an example, run the System Information utility. Keep pressing ↓ until you come to a listing called **System Info** (it's under the **Tools** topic, second from the bottom). The Norton command line should say **SYSINFO** (see Figure 1-2).

2. Press Enter to run the program you've selected. The menu disappears and the opening screen for the utility appears. (Figure 1-3 shows the System Information screen that appears when you run the System Information utility. We will explore this program in detail in Lessons 19 and 20.)

3. When you are ready to exit the utility, hold down the Alt key and press Q (if you are using a mouse, place the cursor on **Quit!** in the menu bar and click the left button). This restores the main Norton menu.

Quitting Norton

To exit the Norton menu, do the following:

- If you are using a mouse, place the cursor over **Quit!** in the menu bar and click the left button.

- From the keyboard, hold down the Alt key and press Q.

In this lesson, you learned how to use the Norton Utilities menu program to run utilities. In the next lesson, you will learn how to run programs from the DOS prompt.

Command line

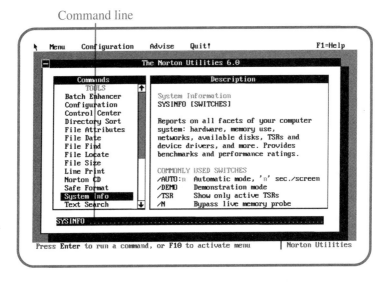

Figure 1-2. Selecting the System Information utility.

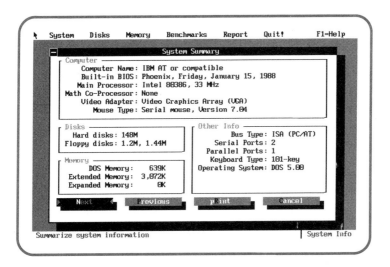

Figure 1-3. The System Information screen showing the System Summary.

Lesson 2

Running Utilities from the DOS Prompt

In this lesson, you will learn the basic rules and terminology for running the Norton utilities from the DOS prompt.

Most of the Norton utilities can be run in either of two ways: *full-screen mode* or *command line mode*.

Full-Screen Mode

In full-screen mode, you use pull-down menus and dialog boxes to select the options that control how the program works (see Lesson 3, "Norton Utilities Basics," for information on using menus and dialog boxes).

To run a utility in full-screen mode, you must start it without any switches or parameters (see definitions in "Understanding Important Terms" later in this lesson). To run a utility in full-screen mode, either select the command from the Norton menu or enter only its *startup command* at the DOS prompt. (See the inside back cover of this book for a summary of the startup commands.) For example, you would enter **disktool** at the DOS prompt to display the opening screen for the Disk Tools utility (see Figure 2-1).

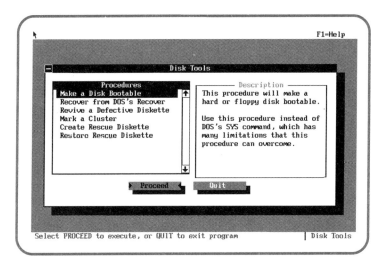

Figure 2-1. The opening screen for Disk Tools.

Command Line Mode

In command line mode, you enter the *program startup command* and the required *parameters* and *switches* at the DOS prompt. This command often resembles the name of the utility's program file. Adding parameters or switches enables you to control the program's operation and bypass the program's opening screen. For example, if you enter the command **disktool /makeboot** at the DOS prompt, The Norton Utilities skips both the opening screen and the Disk Tools menu and takes you right to the Make a Bootable Diskette dialog box (see Figure 2-2).

The lessons in this book will show you how to run the utilities in full-screen mode. However, some lessons will show you how to run the utility in command line mode, and will provide a table showing the switches and parameters

7

available for each utility. Consult your Norton Utilities User's Guide for information about running other utilities in command line mode.

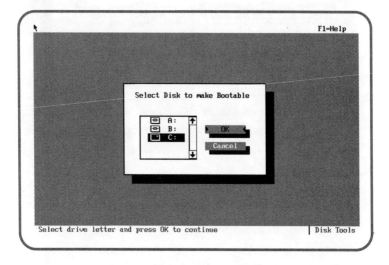

Figure 2-2. The Make a Bootable Diskette dialog box.

Why Run Utilities in Command Line Mode?

The full-screen mode gives you an interface that is easy to use and saves you the bother of having to learn complicated command lines. The price you pay for this comfort is the extra time it takes to select options from the various parts of the screen. The command line is much quicker in most cases because you specify your options in advance. As you become an experienced user of The Norton Utilities, you may find that you prefer the speed of the command line over the ease of use of the full-screen mode.

Understanding Important Terms

Before proceeding, you should become familiar with some of the terms used to describe the various elements that make up the commands you enter. The following terms will be used in the rest of this lesson:

- **Command** An instruction typed at the DOS prompt that tells the computer to run a specific Norton Utilities program in a certain way. The first part of the command consists of the name of the program file. For example the name of the System Information program file is SYSINFO.EXE. To run the program, you type sysinfo and press Enter. The command is refined by adding parameters and switches (explained below) to control how the program works.

- **Syntax** The rules that specify how you enter a command. Syntax tells you things like what order to enter the elements of a command and the proper spelling of the elements.

- **Parameter** A variable element of the command line. File names and disk drive letters are examples of parameters. For example, in the command sformat a:, a: is a parameter.

- **Switch** An optional element of the command line that controls how the program executes. The switch says, in effect, "run the program in this manner." For example, in the command sformat a: /360, /360 is a switch.

Using Global Switches

Most of the Norton utilities have unique switches that do not apply to any of the other programs. There are several

9

switches, however, that you can use with all the utilities. Table 2-1 summarizes these global options.

Table 2-1. Global command line switches.

Switch	Description
/BW	Sets the video for a monochrome display.
/HERC	Sets the video for a Hercules Graphics adapter.
/LCD	Sets the video for a laptop LCD display.
/G0	Disables the graphic mouse and graphic characters on an EGA or VGA display.
/G1	Disables the graphic mouse only on an EGA or VGA display.
/G2	Disables graphic dialog boxes on an EGA or VGA display.
/NOZOOM	Disables dialog box zooming.
/MULTITASK	Disables the check for a multitasking environment.

As an example, if you wanted to run the main Norton program on a laptop computer, you would type **norton /lcd** at the DOS prompt. (Most of the switches in this table can be set automatically by using The Norton Utilities' configuration program NUCONFIG; see Lesson 4, "Configuring the Utilities.")

Command Line Help

You can get help on startup command syntax and switches at the DOS prompt. Simply type the startup command of the utility followed by a forward slash and a question mark. For example, to display command line help for the main Norton

program, type norton /?. The Norton Utilities displays the
syntax and available switches for the program. The help
screen for running Disk Tools is shown in Figure 2.3.

```
C:\>disktool /?
Disk Tools, Norton Utilities 6.0, Copyright 1991 by Symantec Corporation

Six tools for data protection and recovery.

DISKTOOL [/MAKEBOOT] [/SKIPHIGH]
DISKTOOL [/DOSRECOVER] [/SKIPHIGH]
DISKTOOL [/REVIVE] [/SKIPHIGH]
DISKTOOL [/MARKCLUSTER] [/SKIPHIGH]
DISKTOOL [/SAVERESCUE!/RESTORE] [/SKIPHIGH]

    /MAKEBOOT       Make a disk bootable.
    /DOSRECOVER     Recover from DOS's RECOVER command.
    /REVIVE         Revive a defective diskette.
    /MARKCLUSTER    Mark a cluster.
    /SAVERESCUE     Create a Rescue diskette.
    /RESTORE        Restore from a Rescue diskette.
    /SKIPHIGH       Skip using high memory.

C:\>
```

Figure 2-3. The help screen for running Disk Tools.

In this lesson, you learned how to run The Norton
Utilities programs from the DOS prompt. In the next lesson,
you will learn the basics of the Norton Utilities screens.

Lesson 3
Norton Utilities Basics

In this lesson, you will learn basic keyboard and mouse techniques that you can use for all of the Norton Utilities programs.

Elements of The Norton Utilities Screens

The screens of each Norton Utilities program are designed to give you easy access to all the program options. Figure 3-1 shows a typical Norton Utilities screen. It contains two features that are common to all Norton Utilities programs.

- **Pull-Down Menus** The menu bar that runs along the top of the screen contains the pull-down menus. These are hidden menus that appear only after you select one of the items in the menu bar.

- **Dialog Boxes** These boxes pop up on the screen to ask you for information or to seek confirmation of an action you requested. The various elements of a dialog box are called *controls*. Similar controls are sometimes grouped together to create a *control group*. (For example, in Figure 3-1 the three buttons labeled **Start**, **View**, and **Go To** form a control group).

12

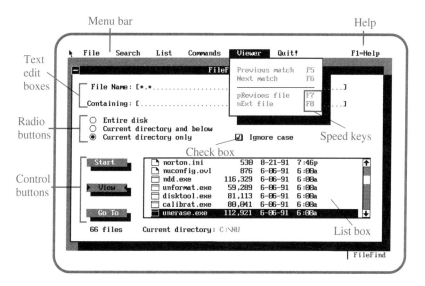

Figure 3-1. Elements of a Norton Utilities screen.

Screen Controls

Figure 3-1 also shows many of the elements of utility screens and dialog boxes you use to perform an action. These controls are:

- **Text Edit Boxes** These are screen areas that allow you to enter text information such as a file name.

- **Radio Buttons** The name for these controls comes from the older car radios where you push in a button to select a station. Pressing a car radio button automatically releases any other button. Similarly, you can only select only one radio button in a control group.

- **Check Boxes** These are simple on-off switches. If the box contains an **X** (or a check mark), the option is enabled; if the box is blank, it is disabled. You can select more than one check box in a group.

13

- **Control Buttons** Control buttons are used to initiate or complete an action.

- **List Boxes** These boxes display lists of items such as file names or directories.

The sections that follow use examples based on the screen shown in Figure 3-1. To try the examples, you can activate this screen by starting the Norton menu program (refer to Lesson 1, "Starting and Exiting the Norton Menu Program"), then selecting the File Find program.

All of the elements of the Norton Utilities screens can be accessed using either the keyboard or the mouse. In the following sections, you will learn how to use the keyboard to navigate the screen.

Selecting Pull-Down Menu Commands with the Keyboard

Entering a command from a pull-down menu is a two-step process. First you pull down the menu, then you select a command. To pull down a menu using the keyboard,

1. Press the Alt key or the F10 key to activate the first pull-down menu. On the File Find screen, the File menu is pulled down.

2. Use ← or → to move to the other menus. Each time you press an arrow key, the previously selected menu disappears and the next menu is pulled down.

3. Press Esc to close a menu.

Quick Menu Access Hold down the Alt key and press the first letter of any menu name to activate that menu. Note that this shortcut only works if no other menu is activated.

The Quit! Menu Option Many Norton Utilities screens have a **Quit!** menu bar option. There is no associated pull-down menu for this option so pressing Alt-Q exits the program.

Once a menu is pulled down, you can select an option from the menu. Each menu option has one letter that is capitalized and appears in a different color. Pressing this letter when the menu is pulled down selects the command.

Menu Speed Keys

You can bypass the pull-down menus and get immediate access to many of the menu options by using certain key combinations or by pressing a *function key*. These key combinations or function keys are listed in the menus to the right of the command (see Figure 3-1). Note that the menu speed keys work only if no menu is activated.

Function Keys Function keys are the keys labeled F1, F2, etc. on your keyboard. These keys provide you with access to commands and special program functions. For example, you can call up the Norton Help screens in any Norton program by pressing the F1 key.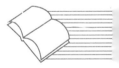

Navigating Dialog Boxes with the Keyboard

Dialog boxes contain a cursor or selection bar that indicates the control or control group you are currently working with. Table 3-1 explains the keys you use to move the cursor or selection bar in the dialog boxes.

Table 3-1. Keys for navigating dialog boxes.

Press	To
Tab	Move to the next control or control group.
Shift-Tab	Move to the previous control or control group.
↑ ↓ → ←	Move to the nearest control or control group in the direction of the arrow.
Home or Page Up	Move to the first control.
End or Page Down	Move to the last control or control group.
Enter	Execute the currently selected control.

Text Edit Boxes

Enter text directly into the field provided. Use the Backspace, Delete, ← and → keys to edit the text.

Radio Buttons and Check Boxes

Once you've moved to a group of radio buttons, use the space bar to change the selected item in a group; only one radio button per group can be selected. A small dot appears inside the button to indicate it's on. When working with check boxes, pressing the space bar turns the selected check box on or off (an option is selected when an **X** or a check mark appears inside its check box). With check boxes, you *toggle* the option on or off; that is, if the option is on, selecting it again turns it off. You can select more than one check box in a group.

List Boxes

List boxes offer a group of choices, such as a list of files. You'll often need to select a list box item by moving the selection bar to it before you select a command button to perform the operation. Use the keys described in Table 3-2 to move around in list boxes.

Table 3-2. Keys to move the selection bar in list boxes.

Press	To Move the Selection Bar
↑ ↓	In the direction of the arrow.
Page Up	Up one screenful (a screenful is the height of the list box).
Page Down	Down one screenful.
Home	To the top of the list.
End	To the bottom of the list.

Using the Mouse to Navigate the Screen

The Norton Utilities can be used with any Microsoft-compatible mouse. In this section, you will learn how to use the mouse to navigate the screen.

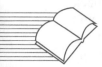

The following terms will be used throughout this book to describe mouse operations:

Point. Move the mouse cursor to an item on the screen.

Click. Press and release the left mouse button, unless told to press the right mouse button.

Double-Click. Press and release either mouse button twice quickly.

Drag. Press and hold down a mouse button while you move the mouse.

Selecting Pull-Down Menu Commands

Follow these steps to access pull-down menus with a mouse:

1. Move the mouse pointer over the menu bar name that you want to select.

2. Click to pull down the menu.

3. Click on a menu item to execute it.

To cancel (close) a pull-down menu, click on a blank area of the screen.

Working with Dialog Boxes

Use the following mouse actions with dialog boxes:

- **Text Edit Boxes** Click on a character in the edit field to move the cursor to that position.

- **Radio Buttons** Click on the button or on its label to select (turn on) the radio button (a radio button is on when a small dot appears inside the button).

- **Check Boxes** Click on the check box or its label to toggle the check box between enabled and disabled (a check box is enabled when an **X** or check mark appears inside the box).

- **Control Buttons** Click on a control button to execute the button. Note that if you click on a control button and keep holding down the mouse button, the control is pressed but not executed. If you continue to hold the mouse button down and then move the mouse off the control, it returns to the unpressed state. This allows you to avoid executing a control button that you have selected by mistake.

- **List Boxes** Click on an item in the list box to select that item. If the list is more than a screenful (that is, there are more items in the list than can be shown), you can use the scroll bars on the right side of the list box to move through the list (see Figure 3-1). Clicking on either scroll bar arrow moves the selection bar in the direction of the arrow.

Getting Help

The Norton Utilities provides context-sensitive help for each screen.

19

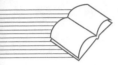 **Context-Sensitive Help** Context-sensitive help means that when you access the Norton help feature, the first help screen will be relevant to the action you are currently performing.

To access the help screens,

- Press F1.

  OR

- Click on F1=Help whenever it appears on the screen. Figure 3-1 shows **F1=Help** in the upper right corner of the screen.

In this lesson, you learned how to navigate the Norton Utilities screens using the keyboard and mouse. In the next lesson, you will learn how to configure The Norton Utilities.

Lesson 4
Configuring the Utilities

In this lesson, you will learn how to use the program NUCONFIG to configure features of The Norton Utilities such as screen colors, passwords, and startup options.

Introducing NUCONFIG

When you installed The Norton Utilities, the installation program established default values for many aspects of the Norton programs. This included hardware options such as setting the video display, and software options such as modifying your system's startup files. (If you chose the Easy configuration during installation, this was all done automatically for you.) Version 6 of The Norton Utilities includes a new program called NUCONFIG which allows you to reconfigure many of these items. So, for example, if you upgrade your video adapter, you do not need to reinstall The Norton Utilities; you simply run NUCONFIG and change the default video option.

Starting NUCONFIG

Start the Norton Utilities configuration program from the DOS prompt by typing **nuconfig** and pressing Enter. The main NUCONFIG screen is displayed, as shown in Figure 4-1.

Accessing Configuration Options with Norton You can also access each of the NUCONFIG options from the Norton menu by pulling down the Configuration menu or by choosing **Configuration** from the menu.

Control buttons   Explanations

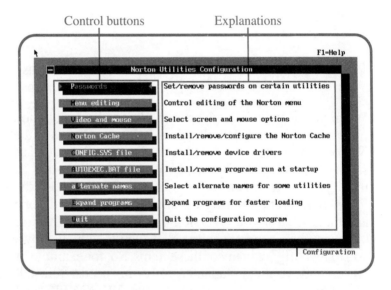

Figure 4-1. The Main NUCONFIG screen.

The main NUCONFIG screen displays nine control buttons running down the left side of the screen. On the right is an explanation for each control button.

22

If you are using a mouse, you select options by clicking on the control buttons. From the keyboard, use ↑ or ↓ to highlight your selection and then press Enter.

Quick Button Access Each of the configuration buttons displays one letter in both upper-case and a different color. Press this letter on your keyboard to execute the option.

Protecting Programs with Passwords

Some of the Norton Utilities programs can seriously damage your system if used improperly or maliciously. To prevent unauthorized use, NUCONFIG allows you to assign a password to 11 of the Norton Utilities programs. **Note:** You can assign only one password for all the programs you select. Follow these steps to assign a password:

1. From the main NUCONFIG screen, select the **Passwords** button. NUCONFIG displays the Password Protection dialog box (see Figure 4-2).

2. If you are using the mouse, click on a check box to select a program for password protection. From the keyboard, move the cursor with the Tab key or the arrow keys and then press the space bar to make a selection. To undo a selection, click on the box or press the space bar a second time.

3. Press Enter when you have chosen all the programs you want to protect. NUCONFIG displays the Set Password dialog box.

4. Type a password in the text field provided. The password can be up to 15 characters consisting of any
combination of numbers and symbols. For added protection, NUCONFIG does not display the password on
the screen as you type. If you enter a blank password,
NUCONFIG will remove a previously assigned password from your selected files.

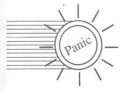

Keep it Simple If you forget your password, you
will NOT be able to use any of the password-
protected programs. To help you remember your
password, keep it short and simple. Use a word that
has some meaning for you.

5. Press Enter or select **OK** to continue. NUCONFIG
displays the Verify Password dialog box. Enter your
password again exactly as you did in Step 4. If you make
a mistake or the passwords do not match, NUCONFIG
will ask you to try again.

6. Press Enter or select **OK**. NUCONFIG assigns the
password to each of the selected programs and returns
you to the main screen.

Controlling Menu Editing

As you learned in Lesson 1, "Starting and Exiting the
Norton Menu Program," most of the Norton Utilities can be
run from the Norton menu. It is also possible to edit the
entries displayed in the Commands window. You can
change or delete existing commands or add your own
commands. This feature is commonly used to set up the
Norton menus for novice or nontechnical users. Programs
considered dangerous or too complex for these users can be
removed. NUCONFIG can then be used to disable the menu

editing capability. Follow these steps to adjust Norton menu editing:

1. From the main NUCONFIG screen, select the Menu editing button. NUCONFIG displays the Norton Menu Editing dialog box.

2. Select either the Enable Editing or Disable Editing radio button.

3. Press Enter or click on OK. NUCONFIG executes the option you selected and returns you to the main screen.

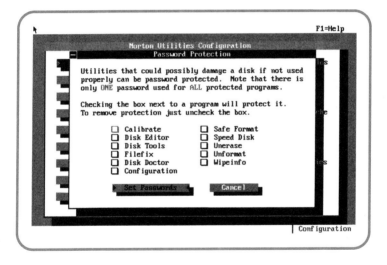

Figure 4-2. The Password Protection dialog box.

Setting Video and Mouse Options

NUCONFIG allows you to adjust the look and feel of The Norton Utilities by setting various options for the display colors, mouse, and screen elements. This part of NUCONFIG is divided into four areas:

- **Screen Colors** You can configure the colors used in the Norton Utilities programs so they display correctly on different types of hardware. You have a choice of laptop colors, black and white or monochrome, and predefined CGA, EGA, or VGA colors. You can also select custom colors.

- **Mouse Options** You can configure your mouse for left- or right-handed use and for use with IBM PS/2 or Compaq mouse ports.

- **Graphics Options** The options in this group allow you to configure the look of various screen elements and the mouse cursor.

- **Screen Options** You can use this group to configure other aspects of the screen, including zooming dialog boxes and the screen background.

To configure the video and mouse options for your computer, follow these steps:

1. From the main NUCONFIG screen, select the Video and mouse button. NUCONFIG displays the Video and Mouse Options dialog box (see Figure 4-3).

2. Select or deselect the appropriate radio buttons or check boxes.

Cannot Select a Button If you find that you cannot activate one of the buttons, you may be trying to select an option that will not run with your hardware. For example, if you have a monochrome display, you cannot select Graphical Dialogs.

3. Press Enter or select Save to execute your selections. NUCONFIG returns you to the main screen.

The Norton Cache

You can perform a basic setup of the Norton Cache program with NUCONFIG. However, this option is recommended only for those who have experience with and fully understand the Norton Cache program. See your Norton Utilities User's Guide for information on using this utility.

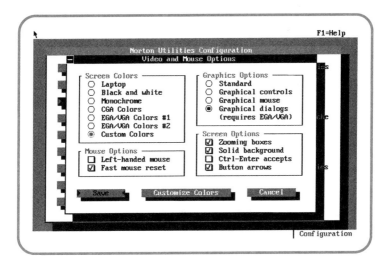

Figure 4-3. The Video and Mouse Options dialog box.

The CONFIG.SYS File Option

The root directory of your hard drive holds a file called CONFIG.SYS. It contains commands that DOS uses to configure your system when you boot up. NUCONFIG allows you to add some of the Norton Utilities commands to this file. However, most of these commands are beyond the scope of this book and we will leave this option to more advanced texts.

Changing Your AUTOEXEC.BAT File with NUCONFIG

NUCONFIG allows you to modify your system's AUTOEXEC.BAT file by adding or deleting Norton Utilities commands.

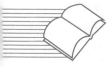 **The AUTOEXEC.BAT File** This is a batch file that resides in the root directory of your hard drive. It contains commands that DOS executes every time you start your computer.

Adding Norton programs to your AUTOEXEC.BAT file means that they will run automatically every time you turn on your computer. This is very important for those utilities that track deleted files, search for virus activity, or check for disk faults. Later lessons will explain how to add utilities to AUTOEXEC.BAT when necessary.

Selecting Alternate Utility Names

NUCONFIG allows you to rename some of the Norton Utilities for added convenience. These include DISKEDIT, SYSINFO, SPEEDISK, FILEFIND, and SFORMAT. Most of the changes involve creating shorter program names which make the programs easier to run from the DOS prompt. For example, if you rename SYSINFO.EXE to

SI.EXE, you can run the system information utility by entering **si** at the DOS prompt. You can also rename the Safe Format program SFORMAT.EXE as FORMAT.EXE to replace the DOS FORMAT.COM program (which is renamed XXFORMAT.EXE). To select alternate names, follow these steps:

1. From the main NUCONFIG screen, select the a**L**ternate names button. NUCONFIG displays the Alternate Program Names dialog box.

2. Select the radio buttons for the program names you wish to use.

3. Click on OK or press Enter to execute the changes. When NUCONFIG has finished renaming the programs, it returns you to the main NUCONFIG screen.

Expanding Programs for Extra Speed

To save disk space, the Norton utilities are stored in compressed form. Each time you use a utility, it is automatically expanded. This process takes only a second or two on most computers but on some slower models it can take as much as six or seven seconds. To eliminate this delay, NUCONFIG can expand the programs to their full size.

Expanding Programs Because the expanded programs can use up to 50% more disk space, you should expand only those programs that you use regularly. Note, too, that you cannot reverse the expansion process, so once files have been uncompressed they must stay that way, unless you reinstall them.

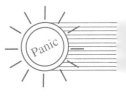

To expand programs from NUCONFIG, follow these steps:

1. From the main NUCONFIG screen, select the **Expand programs** button. NUCONFIG displays the Expand Program Files dialog box that explains the expansion process.

2. Click on **OK** or press Enter to continue. The dialog box displays a listing of the Norton Utilities programs.

3. Select the programs you want to expand by clicking on the program name with the mouse or by highlighting them and pressing the space bar.

4. When you have tagged all the files you want, click on the **Expand** button or press Enter to start the expansion. When NUCONFIG has finished expanding the programs, it returns you to the main NUCONFIG screen.

Quitting NUCONFIG

To quit the configuration program,

1. Select the **Quit** button or press Q. NUCONFIG displays a dialog box asking you to confirm that you want to quit.

2. Press Enter or click on **Yes** to return to DOS.

In this lesson, you learned how to configure The Norton Utilities using the NUCONFIG program. In the next lesson, you will learn how to manage your directories with the Norton Change Directory utility.

Lesson 5
Managing Directories

In this lesson, you will learn how to manage your directories using the Norton Change Directory utility.

Directory Basics

Imagine trying to find a phone number in a telephone directory that was arranged in random order. To help, telephone directories use an alphabetical structure that allows you to find names and phone numbers easily. Likewise, the files on your hard drive can be organized in groups to make them easier to locate, called directories.

The directories on a disk are arranged much like a tree. The "roots" of your system are contained in the aptly named *root* directory. This directory stores the files used by your system to start and configure your computer. Other directories branch off from the root directory. An example is the NU directory, which contains all the Norton Utilities files. Each directory can branch off into several *subdirectories*, which in turn can branch off into additional subdirectories. In such cases, the higher directory is called the *parent* and the subdirectory is called the *descendant*. Any directory or subdirectory can be used to store files.

31

Norton Change Directory

The Norton Change Directory (NCD) program allows you to add, delete, rename, and move through your directories easily by displaying your directory structure graphically in a "tree" diagram.

To start the NCD program type **ncd** at the DOS prompt and press Enter or select the Norton CD command from the Norton menu. The Norton Change Directory main screen appears as shown in Figure 5-1.

Reading the Tree Diagram

The NCD main screen displays your directories graphically in a tree diagram. (The diagram on your computer will likely differ from the one shown in Figure 5-1.) You read the diagram from left to right starting with the backslash (\) in the upper left corner of the tree. The backslash represents the root directory.

No Root Directory? If you do not see the root directory symbol on your display, press the Home key on your keyboard. This moves you to the top of the tree.

The names arranged in the first column to the right of the root (in Figure 5-1, **BATCH, DOS, FONTS**, etc.) are the first level directories. Some of these directories have branches to their right. These are their subdirectories. For example, the **MEMOS** directory has two subdirectories: **BUSINESS** and **PERSONAL**.

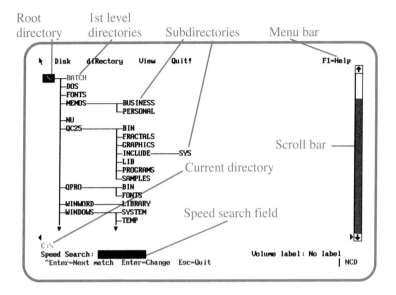

Figure 5-1. The Norton Change Directory main screen.

Navigating Directories

The tree diagram allows you to move easily through your directory structure using either a mouse or keyboard. To navigate directories using a mouse,

- Click on the directory name. NCD highlights the directory name.

- If you have more directories than can be shown on the screen, use the scroll bars to adjust the display up or down.

Use the ↑, ↓, Pg Up, Pg Dn, Home, and End keys to navigate directories from the keyboard.

As you move through the directories, NCD displays the full name of the highlighted directory in the lower left corner of the screen (above the Speed Search field).

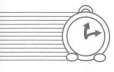

Speed Search Simply type the first few letters of the directory you wish to find in the Speed Search field, and NCD will automatically jump to the first directory name that begins with the letters you typed. Press Ctrl-Enter to find the next directory that matches the letters in the Search field.

Managing Your Directories with NCD

The tree diagram and NCD's pull-down menus make it easy for you to manage your directories. In this section, you will learn how to use NCD to change from one directory to another and to add, delete, and rename your directories.

Changing Drives

If the current drive is not the one you want to work with, follow these steps to change drives:

1. From the main NCD screen, pull down the Disk menu.

2. Select the Change disk option. NCD displays the Select a New Disk dialog box.

3. Choose the drive you want from the list.

4. Select OK. NCD displays the directory tree diagram for the drive you selected.

Changing Directories

Changing directories with DOS is often a slow and cumbersome process because the DOS CD command usually requires you to type the full path to the directory. For example, to change to the subdirectory NOVELS under the directory BOOKS, you would type cd\books\novels. The NCD program makes changing directories quick and easy:

1. From the main NCD screen, select the directory you wish to move to.

2. Press Enter. If you started NCD from the DOS prompt, you are returned to DOS in the directory you selected. If you started NCD from the Norton menu, you are returned to the Norton menu. Simply quit Norton to return to DOS in the selected directory.

Adding a Directory

Follow these steps to make a new directory:

1. From the main NCD screen, highlight the directory that is to be the parent of the new directory.

2. Pull down the diRectory menu.

3. Click on Make or press M. NCD prompts you for the name of the new directory (see Figure 5-2).

4. Enter the name of the directory. The name can be up to 8 characters long and you can add a 3 character extension (separated from the name by a period).

Using Special Characters NCD allows you to use characters normally prohibited by DOS. For example, using NCD you could create a directory called BAD NAME. This name is illegal in DOS because it contains a space and may generate an error if you try to access it using DOS commands. Other characters prohibited by DOS are

+ = / [ ] " : ; , ? * \ < > | .

When you name a directory, try to use only characters accepted by DOS.

5. Click on **OK** or press Enter to create the directory. The new name will appear on the tree diagram and NCD will return you to the main screen.

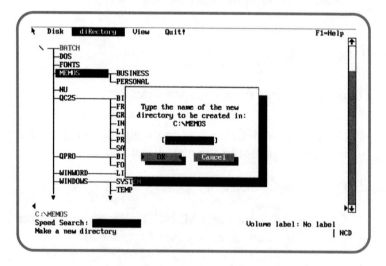

Figure 5-2. Entering the name of the new directory.

Deleting a Directory

Follow these steps to delete directories:

1. From the main NCD screen, highlight the directory you wish to delete.

2. Pull down the diRectory menu.

3. Click on Delete or press D. If the directory is empty, NCD will remove the name from the tree and return you to the main screen. If the directory contains files, NCD will warn you and ask if you are sure you want to delete the directory (see Figure 5-3). Select Yes to erase the files and remove the directory.

Deleting Parent Directories The NCD Delete function will not work on a directory that contains a subdirectory. You must delete any subdirectories first before removing the parent.

Renaming Directories

Follow these steps to rename your directories:

1. From the main NCD screen, highlight the directory you wish to rename.

2. Pull down the diRectory menu.

3. Click on Rename or press R. NCD prompts you for the new name of the directory.

4. Enter the name in the field provided. See "Using NCD to Add a Directory" above for directory naming conventions.

5. Click on **OK** or press Enter to rename the directory. The new name appears on the tree diagram, and NCD returns to the main screen.

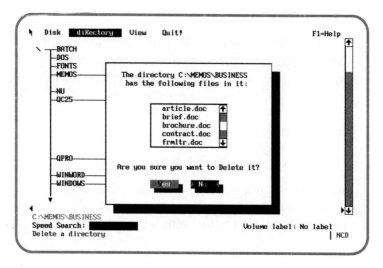

Figure 5-3. The directory to be deleted contains files.

In this lesson, you learned how to manage your directories using Norton Change Directory. In the next lesson, you will learn how to locate and view files.

Lesson 6
Locating and Viewing Files

In this lesson, you will learn how to search for and view files using File Find.

The Need for Search Utilities

Today's large hard disks often contain hundreds or even thousands of files in dozens of directories. Sooner or later, everybody misplaces a file or two and then has to deal with the frustration of searching through all those files and directories.

The Norton Utilities makes finding misplaced files as easy as typing the file name, thanks to File Find. File Find is a full-featured search utility that runs in full-screen mode.

A Primer on Wild-Card Characters

In poker, you can designate one card as "wild"; that card can then assume any value during the game. DOS has borrowed this concept and has designated two symbols, the asterisk (*) and the question mark (?), as *wild-card characters*. The * is used to represent a group of characters in a file name or extension. The ? represents individual characters in a file name or extension. These wild cards play an important role in the File Find and File Locate programs. The following list demonstrates how you can use wild cards:

Wild-Card Entry	Finds
.	All files. This is usually the default entry.
*.DOC	All files with the extension .DOC.
WIN.*	All files named WIN with any extension.
P*.EXE	All files with first letter P and extension .EXE.
???.TXT	All files with three-letter names and extension .TXT.
?DATA.*	All files with names that end with DATA and start with any single letter.
*.?A?	All files where the middle letter of the extension is A.

Using File Find to Search for Files

Follow these steps to run the File Find program and search for a specified file or group of files:

1. If you are using the Norton menu, select File Find from the menu. To run File Find from the DOS prompt, type filefind and press Enter. The Norton Utilities displays the main File Find screen as shown in Figure 6-1.

2. Enter the name of the file you want to find in the File Name text field. You can enter the exact file name or use wild-card characters.

3. Click on the **Start** button or press Enter to execute the search. File Find displays all file names that match the entry you typed. A dialog box alerts you when the search is complete.

4. Click on **OK** or press Enter to return to the main File Find screen. The number of files that matched your file name entry is shown in the lower left corner of the File Find dialog box.

5. To return to DOS in the directory containing one of the located files, highlight the directory in the file list and select the **Go To** button.

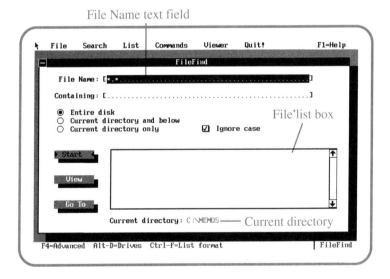

Figure 6-1. The main File Find screen.

Searching Other Drives

You can tell File Find to search for files on other drives. To do this,

41

1. From the main File Find screen, pull down the File menu.

2. Select the Drive option. File Find displays the Change Drive dialog box.

3. Select the drive you want to search from the list box.

4. Select OK to change the drive. File Find returns to the main screen.

5. Execute the search.

Searching Specific Directories

Sometimes you know that a file is in a particular directory or in one of its subdirectories. You can tell File Find to restrict its search to a specific directory or any of its subdirectories by following these steps:

1. From the main File Find screen, pull down the File menu.

2. Select the diRectory option. File Find displays the Change Directory dialog box (see Figure 6-2).

3. Type the name of the directory you want to search in the Current Directory field or select the directory from the Sub-Directories list box.

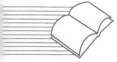

The Parent Directory The Sub-Directories list box may have a listing that is just two dots (..). This symbol represents the parent directory. Selecting this entry moves you up one directory level. For example, the parent of the directory \MEMOS\BUSINESS is \MEMOS.

4. Select **OK** to return to the main File Find screen. File Find displays the new directory name in the Current Directory box.

5. Enter the file name you wish File Find to locate.

6. To restrict the search, select either the **Current directory and below** radio button or the **Current directory only** radio button.

7. Execute the search as explained in the previous section.

Change directory dialog box

Parent directory

Current directory field

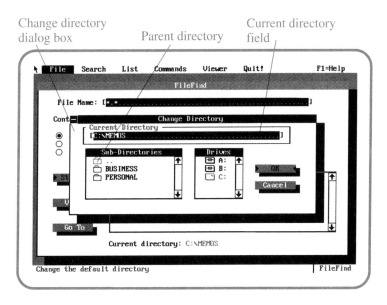

Figure 6-2. The Change Directory dialog box.

Changing the File List Display

By default, the files that File Find displays in the list box are unsorted and each file's name, size, date, time, and attributes (if any) are shown. You may not need this much

43

information, and you may find it easier to locate a file if the list is sorted in some way. To make the file list more manageable, you can change it in any of the following ways:

- **List Format** Controls the type of information displayed for each file. For example, you can choose not to display the date and time the file was created.

- **Sort Criterion** Sorts files by name, extension, date and time, or size. For example, you can sort files by extension to help find all files with the .EXE extension.

- **Sort Order** Sorts the files in ascending or descending order. Ascending is 1 2 3... or A B C...; descending is 10 9 8... or Z Y X....

Follow these steps to modify the file listing:

1. From the main File Find screen, pull down the List menu.

2. Select the Set list display option. The List Display dialog box appears.

3. Select the display options you want by clicking on the appropriate buttons or by using the arrow keys to move the cursor and then pressing the space bar.

4. Click on OK or press Enter. File Find modifies the file listing and returns you to the main screen.

Using File Find to View Files

You can also use File Find to view the contents of the files found during the search. Follow these steps to view a file:

1. Execute a search to get some files displayed in the File Find list box.

2. Click on a file name or use the arrow keys to highlight the file you want to view.

3. Select the View button. File Find displays the contents of the file.

Unusual Characters Don't worry if you see some strange characters or symbols when you view a file. These are usually control codes used by the program that created the file. For example, if you are viewing a file from your word processor, the non-text symbols are used for formatting the document.

4. If you are using a mouse, move through the file by clicking on the scroll bars on the right side of the screen. From the keyboard, use ↑ and ↓ or the PgUp and PgDn keys to scroll through the file.

5. To exit the Viewer and return to the main File Find screen, click on Main! in the menu bar or press Alt-M.

Quick File Finding To find a file from the command line, use the File Locate utility. See your Norton Utilities User's Guide for information.

   In this lesson, you learned how to locate and view files using File Find and File Locate. In the next lesson, you will learn how to search for a file using text strings.

Lesson 7
Searching for Text Strings

In this lesson, you will learn how to use File Find to search for text strings within files.

The Need for Text Searching

In the previous lesson, you learned how to use the Norton Utilities File Find program to locate files by entering some or all of the file's name. It often happens, however, that you cannot remember anything about the name of a file but you do recall some of its contents. By searching for unique text within the file, you could find the file.

Another use for a text search would be to find all your files that mention a particular subject. For example, suppose you have a number of business memos, but you want examine only those memos that discuss a client called Acme Corporation. In this case, you want to be able to generate a list of these files by running a text search on the word "acme."

To accomplish these tasks, you can once again use the File Find utility.

Using File Find for Text Searching

To use the File Find program to search for text strings within files, follow these steps:

1. Run File Find from the Norton menu or from the DOS prompt as explained in Lesson 6. The main File Find screen is displayed.

2. Press Tab or click in the Containing text field. File Find highlights the field.

3. Enter the search text. Note that the search string may contain multiple words or even a partial word. For example, searching for the string "corp" will find words such as "corporate," "corporation," and "corporal."

Keep Search Text Simple Try to keep your text search strings as simple as possible. You will achieve best results if you use a single key word from the text.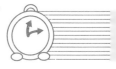

4. Select the Start button to execute the search. File Find displays the files that contain your search string in the list box and shows the number of occurrences of the string in each file (see Figure 7-1).

5. A dialog box appears indicating the completion of the search. Click on OK or press Enter. File Find returns you to the main screen.

6. To go to the directory containing one of the located files, highlight the directory in the File Find list box and select the Go To button. File Find returns you to DOS in the selected directory.

Text string   Files containing   Occurences of
for searching   search string   the string in
                                               each file

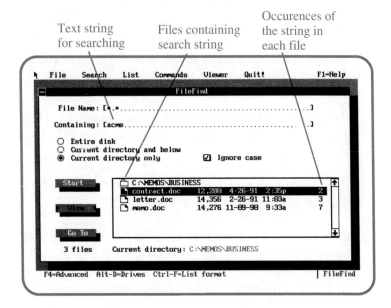

Figure 7-1. Searching for a text string in a file.

Restricting the Text Search

To speed up the search process, you can restrict the search domain to specific directories (see Lesson 6, "Locating and Viewing Files," for information on specifying a search directory). You can also restrict your searches to certain types of files. For example, you may want to search for text only in your word processor files. If these all have, say, a .DOC extension, then you could enter *.DOC in the File Name field, as explained in Lesson 6.

For more accurate text searching, you can ask File Find to distinguish between uppercase and lowercase. For example, you may want to distinguish between the name "Bill" and the word "bill." To do this, simply turn off the Ignore case check box on the main File Find screen.

Searching for Text Strings from the DOS Prompt

To search for a text string from the DOS prompt, type the following:

ff *pathname searchtext [switches]*

where **ff** is the command that runs the File Find utility.

pathname includes the drive, directory, subdirectories, and wild-card entries you want to use in the search (for example, *c:\forest\trees\maple.**). This entry will help narrow the search. You must include a file name.

searchtext is the text string you want to search for.

switches are optional entries which specify how you want the Text Search utility to perform the search. Table 7-1 lists the available switches.

Table 7-1. File Find text search switches.

Switch	Description
/CS	Makes the search case sensitive.
/C	Searches the current directory.
/S	Searches the subdirectories.

For example, the command **ff** **.** **acme** /s will search all files in the current directory and its subdirectories, for the text string ACME. The File Find main screen appears showing the results of the search.

Lesson 8
Setting File Attributes

In this lesson, you will learn how to work with file information such as the date, time, and size of the file and its attributes.

File Attributes

For each file on your computer, DOS keeps track of several pieces of information: its name, size, and the date and time of the last modification. DOS also keeps track of each file's attributes—the settings that indicate the status of the file. Table 8-1 summarizes the four attributes.

Table 8-1. The file attributes.

Attribute	Meaning When Set
Archive	The file has been modified since it was last backed up.
Hidden	The file is not visible to the DIR command.
Read-only	The file cannot be modified or deleted.
System	The file is an operating system file.

You can use the file attributes to help protect important files. For example, you can set the read-only attribute on files to prevent them from being changed or erased. You can use the hidden attribute to keep a file from showing up in a directory listing and away from prying eyes.

Setting File Attributes

As you have learned in the last two lessons, the Norton Utilities File Find program allows you to locate and view files anywhere on your system using either a partial file name or a text string. But File Find can do much more than that. To use File Find to view file attributes:

1. Start the File Find program as explained in Lesson 6.

2. From the main File Find screen, pull down the List menu.

3. Select the Set list display option. File Find displays the List Display dialog box.

4. In the List Format group, select the Name and Attributes radio button to see both the file name and its attributes in the main screen's file list box.

5. Select OK to return to the main File Find screen.

6. Execute a search to display some files in the list box. File Find displays the file name and its attributes as shown in Figure 8-1:

   Arc = archive   **sys** = system
   R/O = read-only   **hid** = hidden

51

Attributes

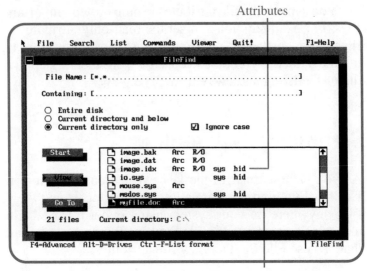

Select a file to change its attributes

Figure 8-1. The file list showing file attributes.

Once a file's attributes are displayed, you can change any of the attributes. To change a file's attributes:

1. Select a file in the list box. For example, the file MYFILE.DOC, which has only its archive attribute set, is selected in Figure 8-1.

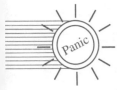

Read-Only and System Attributes Do not try to change files that have their read-only or system attributes set. You could accidentally erase or over-write these files and damage your system.

2. Click on **Commands** in the menu bar or press Alt-C to pull down the Commands menu.

3. Select the **set Attributes** option. File Find displays the Change Attributes dialog box.

52

4. To set or clear attributes, select the appropriate check box. Figure 8-2 shows MYFILE.DOC after clearing the archive attribute and setting the hidden attribute.

5. Select **OK** to modify the attributes. File Find displays a dialog box summarizing changes made to the file.

6. Select **OK** to return to the main screen. File Find displays the file's new attributes in the list box.

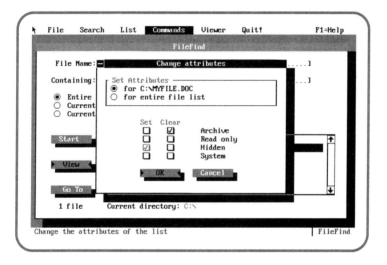

Figure 8-2. The Change Attributes dialog box.

Using the File Attributes Utility

The File Attributes program allows you to view and set attributes quickly from the DOS prompt. (You can also run File Attributes from the main Norton program). At the DOS prompt, type **fa** *pathname [switches]*

where **fa** is the command that runs the File Attributes utility.

pathname includes the drive and directory that contains the files whose attributes you want to change and a wild-card entry specifying the group of files. If you don't specify a directory, File Attributes works only in the current directory.

switches are optional entries which specify how you want the File Attributes utility to perform. Table 8-2 lists the available switches.

Table 8-2. Switches for the File Attributes utility.

Switch	Description
/A[+l–]	Turns the archive attribute on (+) or off (–).
/HID[+l–]	Turns the hidden attribute on (+) or off (–).
/R[+l–]	Turns the read-only attribute on (+) or off (–).
/SYS[+l–]	Turns the system attribute on (+) or off (–).
/DIR	Hides directories.
/CLEAR	Clears all file attributes.
/P	Pauses after each screen.
/S	Includes subdirectories in the command.

For example, the command **fa /hid+** hides all files in the current directory (note that you can omit the file specification; this is equivalent to typing ***.***). To remove the archive attribute from all files with the extension .DOC, type **fa *.doc /a–**.

You can refine your File Attributes commands by combining switches. For example, the command **fa *.exe /hid/r+** makes all the hidden files in the current directory with a .EXE extension read-only.

Changing the File Date and Time

Another piece of information that DOS stores for each file is the date and time the file was created or last modified. DOS provides no easy way of changing these values; fortunately, The Norton Utilities does. This is useful if, for example, you want to adjust the date and time of a file created using DOS's COPY command. When DOS copies a file, it gives the original file's date and time stamp to the new file. It is often beneficial to give the new file a date that reflects when it was created. Controlling the date of a file is also useful if you use a backup program that archives files based on date and time.

Setting the File Date with File Find

The File Find program allows you to change a file's date and time stamp. To change the file date and time:

1. Start the File Find program as explained in Lesson 6.

2. From the main File Find screen, execute a file search to display some files in the list box.

3. Select a file in the list box.

4. Click on **Commands** in the menu bar or press Alt-C to pull down the Commands menu.

5. Select the **set Date/Time** option. File Find displays the Set Date/Time dialog box (see Figure 8-3).

6. By default, the Set Date/Time dialog box displays today's date and time. To accept either of these settings,

click on the appropriate check box. To change these settings, highlight the date or time field and enter the value you want.

7. Click on **OK** or press Enter to execute the changes. File Find displays a dialog box summarizing the changes made.

8. Click on **OK** or press Enter to return to the main File Find screen.

 **Quick Date Changes** You also can change a file's date from DOS with the File Date Utility. See your Norton Utilites User's Guide for information.

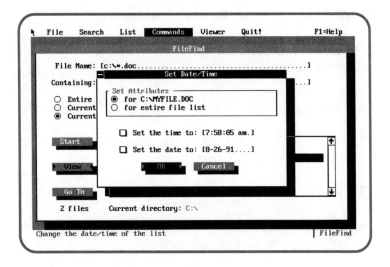

Figure 8-3. The Set Date/Time dialog box.

Determining File Size

When you enter DOS's DIR command, DOS reports the size of each file. What DOS does not tell you is how much space each file takes up. You might think that these values are the same, but they usually are not. The reason is that DOS, in order to work with data efficiently, stores files in fixed-size chunks of disk space called *clusters*. A cluster is the minimum amount of space that DOS will use for a file. So, for example, if a disk has 2,048-byte clusters (the size of a cluster depends on the disk), then even a 1 byte file will take up all 2,048 bytes of disk space. The difference between the cluster size and the file size is called the *slack*.

Determining file *size* is an important consideration if you are copying files to a disk. You need to know if there is enough room on the disk for the files you want to copy. It is not enough simply to add up the respective sizes of the files. You need to know how much slack the files contain and how much slack there will be on the target disk (which may have a different cluster size).

Using File Find to Determine File Size

Once again, the File Find program can do the job. To use File Find to calculate file size, follow these steps:

1. Start File Find as explained in Lesson 6.

2. From the main File Find screen, execute a search to display some files in the list box.

3. Click on Commands in the menu bar or press Alt-C to pull down the Commands menu.

4. Select the Target fit option. File Find displays the Target Fit dialog box.

5. Choose a target drive from the list box.

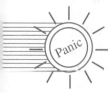

Floppy Drive Target If you choose a floppy disk as your target drive, make sure you insert a formatted disk in the drive before moving on to the next step.

6. Select OK to continue. File Find takes a second or two to calculate the sizes and displays a report that shows the size and slack of the source files and the space needed on the target disk. The report concludes by telling you whether or not there is enough disk space on the target disk for the source files.

7. Select OK to return to the main File Find screen.

Know File Sizes in a Flash To find the size of one or more files from the DOS prompt, run the File Size utility from the DOS prompt. See your User's Guide for information.

In this lesson, you learned how to set the attributes, date, and time for a file and to determine the size of a file. In the next lesson, you will learn how to use The Norton Utilities to print a file from the DOS prompt.

Lesson 9
Printing a File from the DOS Prompt

In this lesson, you will learn how to use the Line Print program to print your text files from the DOS prompt.

Printing from the DOS Prompt

It is often desirable to get a quick printout of a file. You may want to keep a hard copy of important files such as AUTOEXEC.BAT, CONFIG.SYS, or some commonly used batch files. You may want to print out a small "readme" file from a software package or even the program's documentation. If you are a programmer, you may want to print a program listing.

You could use the DOS PRINT command to accomplish these tasks, but PRINT has no formatting capabilities. Instead, you can use the Norton Utilities Line Print program. Line Print can print your text files with a number of formatting options including line numbers, headers, and margins.

Using Line Print

Line Print works only in command line mode from the DOS prompt or from the main Norton program. Figure 9-1 shows an example of a command typed at the DOS prompt. The command syntax is

lp *pathname [output device] [switches]*

where **lp** is the command that runs the Line Print program.

pathname is the drive and directory that contains the file you want to print and the name of the file. You can use wild cards as part of the file name to make Line Print print multiple files. For example, the command **lp c:\programs*.bas** will print all files in the PROGRAMS directory with the extension .BAS.

[output device] is the device you want to print to. For most of your printing needs, you will not need to specify an output device, because the default value is PRN, the standard printer device. If needed, you can specify a different device (such as COM1: or LPT2: to specify a printer that's connected to a different port on your computer) or you can even direct the output to a file.

switches are optional entries which specify how you want the Line Print utility to print the file. Table 9-1 lists the available switches.

Table 9-1. Line print switches.

Switch	Description
/HEADER*n*	Sets the type of header.
	n = 0 No header.
	n = 1 Current date and time on first line (default value).
	n = 2 Current date and time plus file date and time on first two lines.

Switch	Description
/N	Turns line numbering on.
/TAB*n*	Sets TAB size, in spaces (by default, *n* = 8 spaces).
/S*n*	Sets line spacing (by default, *n* = 1 line).
/P*n*	Sets starting page number (by default, *n* = 1).
/T*n* /B*n*	Sets Top and Bottom margins in lines (by default, *n* = 3 lines).
/L*n* /R*n*	Sets Left and Right margins in spaces (by default, *n* = 5 spaces).
/80 or /132	Sets column print width (for IBM-compatible printers only).
/WS	Prints WordStar files.
/PS	Generates output for a PostScript printer.

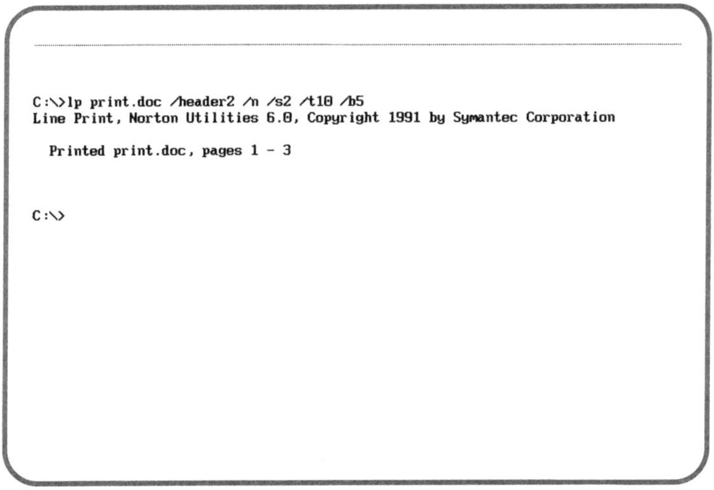

```
C:\>lp print.doc /header2 /n /s2 /t10 /b5
Line Print, Norton Utilities 6.0, Copyright 1991 by Symantec Corporation

  Printed print.doc, pages 1 - 3


C:\>
```

Figure 9-1. Running Line Print from the DOS prompt.

For example, the command **lp readme.txt /s2** prints the file README.TXT with double spacing. If you type **lp *.bat bigbat.txt /header2**, Line Print prints all files in the current directory with the extension .BAT to the file BIGBAT.TXT. For each file, a header is added containing today's date and time as well as the file date and time.

The command **lp \programs\myprog.* lpt2:** prints all files in the PROGRAMS directory with the name MYPROG to the device connected to the LPT2: port.

In this lesson, you learned how to print text files from the DOS prompt using the Line Print utility. In the next lesson, you will learn how to use the Norton Utilities UnErase program to recover deleted files.

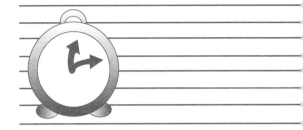

Lesson 10
Recovering Files with UnErase

In this lesson, you will learn how to search for and recover erased files.

Understanding UnErase

There are two types of computer users: those who have accidentally deleted files and those who will. In the past, a deleted file was gone for good. Then came The Norton Utilities and the UnErase program which, under certain conditions, enabled you to recover deleted files.

How is it possible to unerase a file? For every file on a disk, DOS maintains a directory entry and a record of where the contents of a file is physically located on the disk. This record is called the *file allocation table* (FAT).

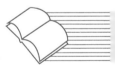

File Allocation Table (FAT) The FAT contains information that tells DOS which clusters on a disk are being used and which are available for use. The FAT keeps track of where each file's clusters are located on the disk.

When you issue the DEL or ERASE command, DOS does not remove the contents of the file from the disk.

Instead, DOS simply makes the disk areas occupied by the file available to the system for storing other files. It does this by setting the file's FAT entries to zero and by replacing the first letter of the file name (in the directory entry) with a special character. All you need to do (with the help of UnErase) is restore that first letter.

When Should You Use UnErase?

You should use UnErase immediately after deleting a file. This reduces the chance that DOS will overwrite the erased file's sectors with another file. If you accidentally erase a file and then execute several other move and copy operations, your chances of recovering the deleted file are greatly reduced.

Using UnErase before Installation The Norton Utilities installation process may overwrite erased files. If you've accidently deleted files but have not yet installed The Norton Utilities, don't install The Norton Utilities now. Insert The Norton Utilities Emergency Disk in drive A or drive B (if you're using 5.25" diskettes, use Emergency Disk #2). Type **a:unerase** or **b:unerase**. Then proceed with steps 2 through 5 of the recovery procedure, described in the next section.

Using UnErase to Recover Files

Perform the following steps to unerase a deleted file.

1. Type **unerase** at the DOS prompt and press Enter or start the UnErase utility from the Norton menu.

2. The UnErase program displays a list of deleted files in the current directory (see Figure 10-1). You may need to change directories to display the directory with the files you want to restore. See the next section to learn how to do so.

3. Highlight the file you want to unerase by clicking on it or by using ↑ or ↓.

4. Click on the UnErase button (or press U). UnErase displays a dialog box giving information about the deleted file and prompting you for the first letter of the deleted file's name.

5. Enter the first letter of the file's name. UnErase closes the dialog box and returns to the file list display. The message **RECOVERED** appears beside the recovered file.

6. Repeat steps 3 to 4 to unerase other files in the same directory.

Listing Files in Other Directories

The UnErase program offers several methods for displaying erased files in other directories:

- Some of the entries that UnErase displays show **DIR** in the Size column. These entries are directories. Highlight one of these entries and press Enter or double click on it to display the erased files in that directory.

- Click on File (or press Alt-F) and select view All directories to display all erased files. (Or, simply press Alt-A.)

Current directory

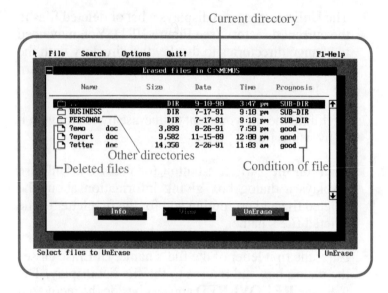

Figure 10-1. The UnErase screen.

- Click on **File** (or press Alt-F) and select **change diRectory** to view the Change Directory dialog box with a tree listing of directories. With the mouse, use the scroll bar to move through the tree. Double click on the directory to display the erased files. If you are using the keyboard, press ↑ or ↓ or the Page Up and Page Down keys to scroll through the tree. Press Enter to choose a directory.

Speed Search Type the first few letters of the subdirectory you wish to access in the Speed Search box, and UnErase will automatically jump to the first directory name containing the letters you typed. To move to the next directory name matching the letters in the Search field, press Ctrl-Enter.

Searching for Deleted Files

You may not remember the name of a deleted file or even which directory the file was in. It is even possible that the directory itself has been deleted. For these situations, UnErase offers three types of file searches: searching for Data Types, searching for Text, and searching for Lost Names. Pull down the Search menu and choose one of those options to locate the file you want to unerase. Once you have found the file you want to unerase using these searches, you can then proceed to recover the file.

Selecting Multiple Files to Unerase

To speed the unerase procedure, you can unerase several files at once. UnErase lets you select files one by one or in a group.

Selecting and Recovering Files Individually

If the files you want to unerase have very different names, use the following procedure to select them individually:

1. At the main UnErase screen, highlight the name of the file you want to unerase and press the space bar. An arrow appears to the left of the selected file. (Alternatively, you can choose the Select option from the File menu.)

2. Move the highlight to the name of the next file you want to unerase and press the space bar to select it. Repeat this step to select as many files as you wish.

3. Select **UnErase**. UnErase displays a dialog box with the message **Attempt to recover x files?** where x is the number of files you selected.

4. Click on **UnErase** or press Enter to confirm that you want to unerase multiple files. UnErase displays a dialog box giving information about the first deleted file and prompting you to supply the first letter of the deleted file's name.

5. Enter the first letter of the file's name. UnErase displays the information for the next file. Continue entering the first letter for each file. When you have gone through all the selected files, UnErase closes the dialog box and returns to the file list display.

Selecting and Recovering a Group of Files

If you accidently deleted a group of files, using a command like erase *.doc, you can use the UnErase utility to recover that same group of files. UnErase lets you enter wild-card characters to perform such an operation.

Wild Cards If you do not know how to use wild cards to work with groups of files, refer to the section "A Primer on Wild-Card Characters" in Lesson 6.

Take the following steps to recover a group of files:

1. At the main UnErase screen, pull down the File menu and choose the **select Group** option or press the + key on your numeric keypad. If you make a mistake, you can undo your selection by choosing **Unselect group** from the File menu or by pressing the – key on the numeric keypad.

2. Enter the selection criteria in the dialog box (see Figure 10-2). For example, you could type *.doc to select all deleted files with the .DOC extension in the current directory.

3. Click on **OK** or press Enter. UnErase displays arrows beside all the files in the current directory that match your criteria.

4. Select **UnErase**. UnErase displays a dialog box with the message **Attempt to recover *x* files?** where *x* is the number of files selected.

5. Click on **UnErase** or press Enter to confirm that you want to unerase multiple files. UnErase displays a dialog box giving information about the first deleted file and prompting you to supply the first letter of the deleted file's name.

6. Enter the first letter of the file's name. UnErase displays the information for the next file. Continue entering the first letter for each file. When you have gone through all the selected files, UnErase closes the dialog box and returns to the file list display.

69

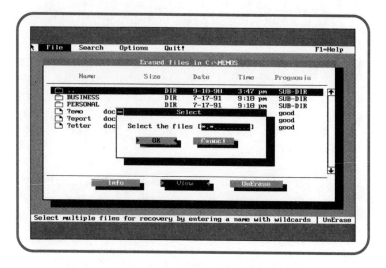

Figure 10-2. The Select Group dialog box.

In this lesson, you learned how to search for and recover erased files. In the next lesson, you will learn how to increase the chances of successfully recovering files using Erase Protect.

Lesson 11
Enhancing File Recovery with Erase Protect

In this lesson, you will learn how to use the Erase Protect program to improve your chances of recovering deleted files.

How Erase Protect Works

In the previous lesson, you learned how to recover files using the UnErase program, as long as the files were not overwritten. But UnErase cannot prevent DOS from writing over a deleted file's sectors. A single COPY command could make it impossible for you to recover a deleted file.

To increase your chances of recovering deleted files, use the Norton Utilities Erase Protect program. Erase Protect runs in your computer's memory and monitors all disk activity. Every time you delete a file, Erase Protect moves the file to a special directory called TRASHCAN. As long as the file's contents remain in the TRASHCAN directory, you can recover the file with 100% reliability. Erase Protect allows you to manage the TRASHCAN directory so it never grows beyond a maximum size and allows you to have the files purged automatically after a certain amount of time.

Using Erase Protect

Follow these steps to run the Erase Protect program:

1. Start Erase Protect either by selecting **Erase Protect** from the main Norton program or by entering **ep** at the DOS prompt. The main Erase Protect screen is displayed as shown in Figure 11-1.

2. Select the **Choose drives** button. Erase Protect displays the Choose Drives dialog box.

3. Select the drive or drives that you wish to protect (you can use Erase Protect on hard drives, floppy drives, and network drives).

4. Select the **ON** button or press Enter. Erase Protect returns you to the main screen, changes the Status line beside the **Choose drives** button to **ON** and displays the number of drives you selected.

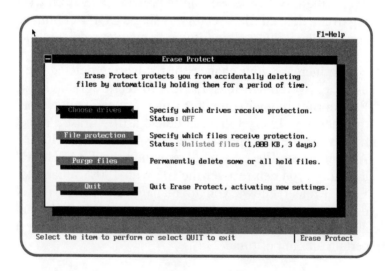

Figure 11-1. The main Erase Protect screen.

Setting File Protection Parameters

You can customize Erase Protect to protect (or exclude from protection) certain files. The following options are available:

All files (*.*)	Protects all files on the drives you selected.
Only the files listed	Protects only those files with the extensions you specify.
All files except those listed	Protects all files except those with the extensions you specify.

For example, you might want to protect only your data files. Thus, you could protect only those files with, say, the .DBF or .WK1 extensions. Conversely, you might want to exclude from protection all .BAK (backup) files or .TMP (temporary) files (especially if you run Windows). You can also choose to include files that have had their archive attribute reset (have been backed up). This option is normally turned off because you can easily restore these files from the backup copies.

Erase Protect can also purge files automatically after a specified length of time and set a maximum size for the TRASHCAN directory. To set these Erase Protect parameters, take the following steps:

1. From the main Erase Protect screen, select the File protection button. Erase Protect displays the File Protection dialog box (see Figure 11-2).

2. Select one of the three radio buttons to specify which files you want to protect. If you choose All files (*.*), skip to Step 5. If you choose either Only the files listed or All files except those listed, enter one or more file extensions (the maximum is nine).

3. Click on the Files list box or press → twice. A highlight appears beside *. in the first line.

4. Enter the file extension. Use the arrow keys to move the highlight and enter more extensions.

5. Click on the Purge files held over [..] days text box or press Tab until the text box is highlighted.

6. Enter the number of days you want Erase Protect to hold files before purging them. Enter 0 for no limit.

7. Click on the Hold at most [....] Kbytes text box or press Tab. Enter the maximum size for the TRASHCAN directory. The amount you enter depends upon the size of the disk and how much free space it has. For example, to set the size of TRASHCAN to 1 megabyte, enter 1000 in the box. Enter 0 for no limit.

8. Select OK or press Enter to return to the main Erase Protect screen. Erase Protect displays your selections on the Status line beside the File protection button.

Purging Protected Files

You can use Erase Protect to purge some or all of the files in the TRASHCAN directory. This is a good idea if a protected drive is running out of room, or if you want to get rid of some unimportant files to make more room for important ones. To use the Erase Protect purge feature, do the following:

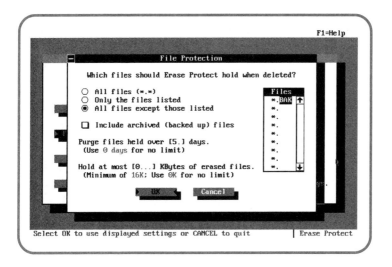

Figure 11-2. The File Protection dialog box.

1. From the main Erase Protect screen, select the **Purge files** button. Erase Protect displays the Purge Deleted Files dialog box (see Figure 11-3).

2. The dialog box displays all the deleted files in the current drive's TRASHCAN directory. To view another drive, select the **Drive** button and choose a drive from the dialog box that appears. Select **OK** to return to the Purge Deleted Files dialog box.

3. To tag a file you want purged, click on the file in the list box or use the arrow keys to move the highlight and press the space bar. To tag a group of files, select the **Tag** button. Enter the file specification in the Tag text box. Select **OK** to return to the Purge Deleted Files dialog box.

4. To purge the files you have tagged, select the **Purge** button. Erase Protect deletes the files from TRASHCAN and returns you to the main Erase Protect screen.

75

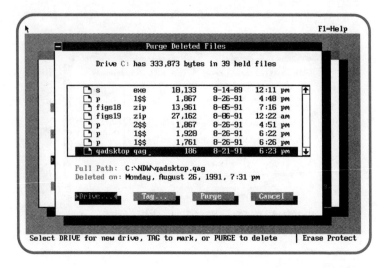

Figure 11-3. The Purge Deleted Files dialog box.

Running Erase
Protect Automatically

To get the maximum benefit from Erase Protect, you should have it running in memory at all times. Ideally, you should load Erase Protect as soon as you start your computer. You can have your system run Erase Protect automatically by including the line **ep /on** in your AUTOEXEC.BAT file (see Lesson 4, "Configuring the Utilities," for an explanation of the AUTOEXEC.BAT file). If you aren't sure how to enter the line, you can have The Norton Utilities do it:

1. Start NUCONFIG by selecting **Configuration** from the Norton menu or by entering **nuconfig** at the DOS prompt and pressing Enter. The Norton Utilities Configuration dialog box appears.

2. Select the **AUTOEXEC.BAT** button. NUCONFIG displays the AUTOEXEC.BAT Setup dialog box.

3. Activate the **Load the Erase Protect Utility** check box.

4. Select **OK** or press Enter. NUCONFIG displays the revised AUTOEXEC.BAT file.

5. Select the **Save** button to accept the changes. NUCONFIG returns you to the main Configuration screen.

6. Quit NUCONFIG by selecting the **Quit** button and selecting **Yes** in the dialog box that appears.

7. Reboot your computer to put the changes you made to your AUTOEXEC.BAT file into effect.

In this lesson, you learned how to enhance file recovery with the Erase Protect utility. In the next lesson, you will learn how to format disks safely using the Norton Utilities Safe Format program.

77

Lesson 12
Formatting Disks Using Safe Format

In this lesson, you will learn how to format a disk using Safe Format.

Formatting Floppy Disks

You must *initialize* your floppy disks before you can use them. This initialization, known as *formatting*, creates an organizational structure on the disk that DOS uses to read and store information.

Before the release of DOS 5.0, FORMAT was one of DOS's riskiest commands because it would wipe out all the data a disk may already contain. In fact, before DOS 3.3, FORMAT would simply initialize the current drive (hard disk or floppy), no questions asked! If you entered **format** at the C:> prompt, DOS would format drive C. Later versions of DOS prompt you for a volume label before formatting a hard drive. DOS 5 has even added new features that allow you to recover from an accidental format. However, DOS still does not warn you if you attempt to format a floppy disk that contains data.

The bottom line is that no matter what version of DOS you use, Norton Utilities Safe Format adds extra levels of protection to help reduce the risk of losing data.

Renaming Safe Format For an added measure of safety, you can rename Safe Format as FORMAT.EXE using The Norton Utilities configuration program NUCONFIG. Doing this effectively replaces DOS's FORMAT.COM (which is renamed XXFORMAT.COM) with Safe Format. See Lesson 4 "Configuring the Utilities" for instructions on how to use NUCONFIG.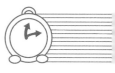

Running Safe Format

Follow these steps to start the Safe Format program:

1. Insert the floppy disk you want to format in the appropriate drive.

2. Select **Safe Format** from the Norton menu or type **sformat** at the DOS prompt and press Enter.

3. The main Safe Format screen appears (see Figure 12-1).

Two of the boxes on the main Safe Format screen—the System Files and Format Mode boxes—offer options that give the Safe Format utility significant flexibility.

The System Files box contains options that determine whether or not Safe Format puts system files (the files that make your computer boot and run) on the disk as it is formatted. You have three options:

Format Size box ─┐   Safe UnFormat Info check box
Disk drive box | Volume Label field | Format Mode box

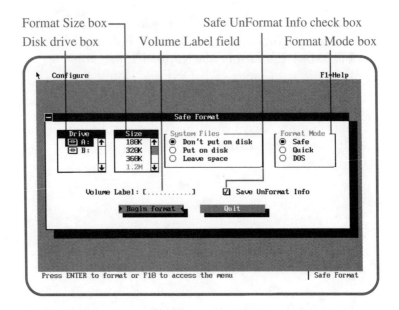

Figure 12-1. The main Safe Format screen.

- **Don't put on disk.** This option creates a non-bootable disk with no room reserved for the system files.

- **Put on disk.** This option creates a bootable disk by placing the system files on the disk. You can use the disk to start your system.

- **Leave space for system files.** This option creates a non-bootable disk with room reserved for the system files. This allows you to make the disk bootable later (using DOS's SYS command, for example) without having to reformat.

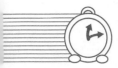

Keep a Bootable Disk You should always have a bootable disk in storage just in case your system gets corrupted and will not boot from your hard drive.

The Format Mode box lets you choose what type of formatting is applied to the floppy disk. You have three format mode options on disks formatted with Safe Format:

* **Safe** In this mode, Safe Format checks the disk to see if it has been previously formatted. If it has, Safe Format displays any files and subdirectories on the disk and asks if you are sure you want to proceed. If you answer Yes, the program resets the system area and checks the physical disk for defects but keeps the data intact. This allows you to UnFormat the disk easily and restore the original information, as long as you don't store any new files on the disk.

* **Quick** You can use this mode only on previously formatted disks. Quick format takes only a few seconds because the program only resets the system area and stores the UnFormat information.

* **DOS** This mode functions much like the DOS FOR-MAT command. The program destroys all the data on a previously formatted disk and you will not be able to UnFormat it.

Formatting a Floppy Disk

Follow these steps to format a floppy disk using Safe Format:

1. In the **Drive** box on the main Safe Format screen, select the drive that contains the disk by clicking on the drive letter or by pressing ↑ or ↓. Notice that the Drive box lists only floppy drives. By default, Safe Format allows you to format only floppy disks.

81

2. Press Tab to move to the Size box and select the format size. See Table 12-1 for a summary of common format sizes and check the disk label or box to determine the density of the floppy disks you have.

3. Press Tab to move to the System Files box. Select the option you want by clicking on the appropriate radio button or using ↑ or ↓ to move to the radio button and then pressing the space bar.

4. Press Tab to move to the Format Mode box and select a format mode.

5. Press Tab to highlight the Volume Label box. You use the volume label to identify your disks. The name can be up to 11 characters long and is optional.

6. Press Tab to highlight the Save UnFormat Info check box. If you check this box, Safe Format will run the IMAGE program before formatting the disk. This allows you to easily UnFormat the disk later should you need to do so. See Lesson 13 "Recovering from an Accidental Format" for details on how IMAGE works.

7. Press Enter to begin formatting.

8. If the disk was previously formatted and contains data and you chose the Safe or Quick mode, Safe Format will show you the files and directories on the disk and ask if you want to proceed. Select Yes to continue.

9. When Safe Format is done, a dialog box appears telling you that the floppy disk was successfully formatted. Click on OK or press Enter to return to the main Safe Format screen.

10. To format another floppy disk using the same options, simply insert the new disk in the drive and press Enter. For a disk that requires different options, repeat steps 1 through 9 above.

Table 12-1. Common disk format sizes.

Disk Size and Capacity	Format Size
3.5" Double Density	720K
3.5" High Density	1.44M
5.25" Double Density	360K
5.25" High Density	1.2M

Using Safe Format with Command Switches

You can specify most of the options in the Safe Format screen by including command switches when you start SFORMAT from the DOS prompt. For example, typing sformat a: /s /v:memos would format the disk in drive A: as a bootable disk and assign it the volume label "MEMOS." Table 12.2 lists some of the switches you can include when you run SFORMAT.

Table 12-2. Command line switches for Safe Format.

Switch	Description
drive:	Specifies the drive letter of disk to format. Replace *drive* with the letter of the drive.
/A	Sets Automatic Mode: Formats without interruption and returns to DOS when done.

continues

83

Table 12-2. (continued)

Switch	Description
/S	Copies the system files to the disk, making it bootable.
/B	Leaves space for the system files.
/V:*label*	Adds a volume label to the disk. Replace *label* with the label you want to use.
/Q	Sets Quick Format mode.
/D	Sets DOS Format mode.
/4	Formats a 360K disk in a 1.2M drive.

In this lesson, you learned how to format a disk using The Norton Utilities' Safe Format. In the next lesson, you will learn how to use UnFormat to recover an accidentally formatted disk.

Lesson 13
Recovering from an Accidental Format

In this lesson, you will learn how to use the UnFormat program to recover an accidentally formatted disk.

Understanding UnFormat

Although Safe Format helps prevent accidental formatting, you may still format a disk by mistake. It is also possible that a computer virus or power surge could damage a disk. To recover your disk in these situations, you can use the UnFormat program.

To understand how UnFormat can restore your formatted disks, you need to know a little about the structure of a disk. Every disk is divided into two areas: the system area and the data area. The *system area* contains a log of the files stored on the disk, where the files are located, what the root directory contains, and booting instructions (if the disk is bootable). The *data area* contains the data and program files you work with.

Safe Format reinitializes the system area but leaves the data area intact. (This is also true if you use the DOS

FORMAT command on a hard disk. On floppy disks, FORMAT wipes the data area.) After formatting, DOS reports that the disk is empty, but your data files are still there for UnFormat to recover. UnFormat first tries to restore the system area. If it cannot, it uses the intact data area to reconstruct the disk. You will obtain the best results if you use UnFormat immediately after formatting a disk.

Use IMAGE to Enhance Disk Recovery

UnFormat always looks for a file called IMAGE.DAT created by the Norton Utilities Image program. This file contains a snapshot of the disk's system area. Recovering a disk is much faster and much more reliable if IMAGE.DAT exists. You will learn how to run the Image utility later in this lesson. If you formatted the disk with Safe Format, and the Save UnFormat Info check box was on (see Lesson 12, "Formatting Disks Using Safe Format"), then Safe Format automatically created IMAGE.DAT for you.

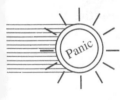

Using UnFormat before Installation If you accidently formatted your hard disk, do NOT install The Norton Utilities now. The Norton Utilities installation program may overwrite files in the data area of your hard disk. To UnFormat a hard disk before installation, insert the Norton Utilities Emergency Disk (if you are using 5.25" disks, use Emergency Disk #2) in drive A or B and enter **a:unformat** or **b:unformat**. Then proceed with steps 2 through 10 of the recovery procedure, described in the next section.

Using UnFormat to Recover Disks

Follow these steps to recover a disk:

1. Start the UnFormat program by either selecting **UnFormat** from the Norton menu or by entering **unformat** at the DOS prompt. The UnFormat dialog box appears.

2. Click on **Continue** or press Enter to remove the UnFormat window. UnFormat displays a dialog box prompting you for the drive letter of the disk.

3. Choose the drive from the list box and select **OK** to continue.

4. UnFormat analyzes the disk you selected and then displays a dialog box that asks you if you used either IMAGE.EXE or MIRROR.COM to save the recovery information for the disk (see Figure 13-1).

   MIRROR.COM is a DOS 5.0 utility that is 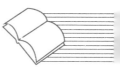 equivalent to the Norton Utilities Image program. UnFormat can use the data from either program to recover a disk.

5. If you are sure that you did not run either of these programs on the disk, select **No** and skip to the section "Recovering a Disk without IMAGE.DAT." Select **Yes** if you ran either of these programs or if you are not sure.

   If there are files on the disk you selected, UnFormat shows a list of the files and asks if you want to proceed. If the disk is empty, UnFormat displays a dialog box that asks you if you are sure you want to UnFormat the disk you selected.

6. Select **Yes** to proceed. UnFormat searches the disk for the IMAGE.DAT file. If UnFormat finds the file, it displays a dialog box that tells you when the information was saved. Select **OK** to continue.

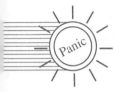

More Than One IMAGE File? If you ran the Image program on a disk more than once, Image backed up the previous IMAGE.DAT file in a new file called IMAGE.BAK. If UnFormat finds both files on the disk, it will ask you which file you want to use. Most of the time, you can select the **Recent** option. You would select the **Previous** button if you suspected that IMAGE.DAT (the most recent file) contained a snapshot of a corrupt disk.

7. UnFormat displays a message warning you that you may lose any changes made to the disk since the last time the Image information was saved. Select **Yes** to proceed.

8. UnFormat now asks you if you want to do a "Full" or "Partial" restoration of the disk. The Full option restores the entire system area, while Partial restores only specific parts of the system area. Select **Full** to start the unformat operation.

9. After a few seconds, UnFormat reports on the results of the recovery. Select **OK**. UnFormat returns you to the UnFormat dialog box.

10. Select the **Quit** button to exit the UnFormat program or select **Continue** to recover another disk.

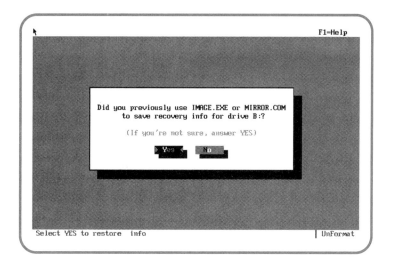

Figure 13-1. Did you save the disk recovery information?

Recovering a Disk without IMAGE.DAT

In Step 4 of the previous section, you saw how UnFormat asks you if you have used Image (or Mirror) to save the disk's system information. Running the Image program is discussed later in this lesson. For now, it is most likely that your disks do not contain unformat information. In this case, follow these steps to complete the disk recovery:

1. After you have told UnFormat that you did not use Image or Mirror (see Step 5 in the previous section), UnFormat displays a dialog box that asks you if you are sure you want to unformat the disk.

2. Select Yes to execute the recovery process. Depending on the type of disk, this may take several minutes or more.

3. When the recovery is complete, UnFormat informs you that it has successfully unformatted the disk. Select **OK** to continue.

4. UnFormat displays a dialog box that recommends you examine the disk to ensure that the recovery was successful. Without IMAGE.DAT, UnFormat cannot restore any directories that were on the disk. Instead, UnFormat creates new directories named DIR0, DIR1, etc. Examine the contents of these directories and then rename them with the Norton Change Directory program (see Lesson 5, "Managing Directories"). Select OK in the dialog box.

Starting Norton Change Directory In this situation, use the command **ncd** /n to start the Norton Change Directory utility. The /N switch tells NCD not to store the current directory information in a disk file.

5. You are returned to the UnFormat dialog box. Select Quit to exit UnFormat or Continue to recover another disk.

Running the Image Program

Running Image is extremely easy. Simply enter the command image [drive:] at the DOS prompt (if you don't specify a drive letter, Image runs on the current drive) or choose the Image command from the main Norton program. That's all there is to it. You should run Image on your hard drive regularly, especially after you've added or changed several files on the disk.

Ideally, you should add the Image command to your
AUTOEXEC.BAT file so it runs automatically every time
you start your computer. You can use the Norton Utilities
configuration program NUCONFIG to do this for you.
Follow these steps:

1. Start NUCONFIG either by selecting Configuration
   from the Norton menu, or by typing nuconfig at the
   DOS prompt and pressing Enter. The Norton Utilities
   Configuration dialog box appears.

2. Select the AUTOEXEC.BAT button. NUCONFIG
   displays the AUTOEXEC.BAT Setup dialog box.

3. Activate the Run the IMAGE Utility check box.

4. Select OK or press Enter. NUCONFIG displays the
   revised AUTOEXEC.BAT file.

5. Select the Save button to accept the changes.
   NUCONFIG returns you to the main Configuration
   screen.

6. Quit NUCONFIG by selecting the Quit button and
   selecting Yes in the dialog box that appears.

7. Reboot your computer to put the changes you made to
   your AUTOEXEC.BAT file into effect.

   In this lesson, you learned how to recover damaged or
accidentally formatted disks. In the next lesson, you will
learn how to remove a file from a disk permanently.

Removing
a File
Permanently

In this lesson, you will learn how to remove a file from a disk permanently using the Wipe Information program.

Why Remove Files Permanently?

Problems can arise when you delete confidential files such as personnel records or top-secret memos. Pieces of these files can remain on your computer for some time. Somebody who knows how to use a utility like UnErase can recover some or all of these sensitive files. To prevent this from happening, The Norton Utilities contains a program called Wipe Information that enables you to permanently remove all traces of a file.

Use Wipe Information with Caution Use the Wipe Information utility with extreme caution. You cannot use UnErase or UnFormat to recover files or drives that you have wiped.

How Wipe Information Works

The idea behind Wipe Information is simple. The program completely overwrites the data area of the file or drive you want wiped using a value that you specify (such as 1 or 0). UnErase or UnFormat cannot restore the file or drive because there is nothing left to restore. Wipe Information can remove files in two ways:

- **Fast Wipe** Writes over the data area once with a single value. The default value is 0, but you can use any ASCII character.

- **Government Wipe** Uses the three-step Department of Defense (DOD) standard for wiping confidential information from disks:

    1. Writes over the data area first with 0s, and then with 1s, at least three times.

    2. Writes over the data area with the character represented by decimal value 246.

    3. Verifies the write in Step 2 to ensure that the original data was completely wiped.

You can configure the Government Wipe to repeat the 0s and 1s up to 999 times and to use another character for the final write.

You may be wondering why the more elaborate Government Wipe is needed. The reason has to do with the technical properties of disk recording heads. A single wipe can still leave a very faint magnetic *fingerprint* on the disk. This file trace is too subtle to be UnErased, but there are highly sensitive devices that can read this information.

Which Method Should You Use?

Fast Wipe will quickly remove your confidential files and keep them from all but the most sophisticated eyes. If your files are extremely sensitive, then you should opt for the peace of mind offered by Government Wipe. Be warned, however, that a Government Wipe of a floppy disk can take up to a couple of hours, while an entire hard disk could take half a day!

Running the Wipe Information Utility

Start the Wipe Information utility either by selecting **WipeInfo** from the main Norton menu, or by entering **wipeinfo** at the DOS prompt. The main Wipe Information screen appears (see Figure 14-1).

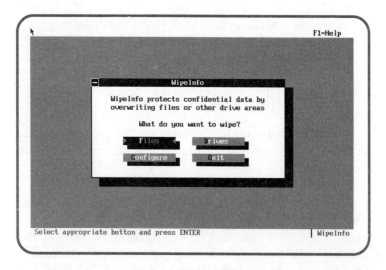

Figure 14-1. The main Wipe Information screen.

Configuring Wipe Information

Follow these steps to configure Wipe Information:

1. From the main Wipe Information screen, select the Configure button. Wipe Information displays the Wipe Configuration dialog box (see Figure 14-2).

2. Select either **Fast Wipe** or **Government Wipe**.

3. If you chose **Fast Wipe**, you can select a different write value (the default is 0). If you chose **Government Wipe**, you can change the number of 0/1 write repeats (the default is 3) and the value of the final write (the default is 246).

4. Press Tab to set the **Repeat count** value (the default is 1). This controls the number of times the wipe is performed.

5. If you would like to use these values for future wipes, select the **Save settings** button. Otherwise, select **OK**. Wipe Information returns you to the main screen.

Using Wipe Information to Permanently Wipe Files

You can ask Wipe Information to wipe a single file, or you can use wild cards and include subdirectories to wipe multiple files. You can even wipe hidden and read-only files. Three methods are available for wiping files:

- **Wipe files.** Wipes the data area used by the files according to the Wipe Configuration.

95

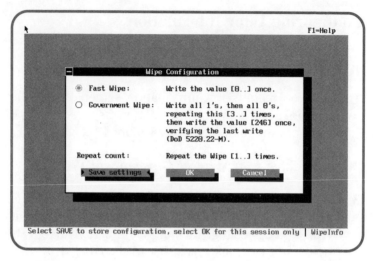

Figure 14-2. The Wipe Configuration dialog box.

- **Delete files only, don't wipe.** Deletes the files just like the DOS commands ERASE or DEL.

Deleting Subdirectory Files The DOS commands DEL and ERASE will delete files only in the current directory. You can use the **Delete files only...** method to delete files in the current directory and all its subdirectories. Simply activate the **Include subdirs** check box in the Wipe Files dialog box (see Figure 14-3).

- **Wipe unused file slack only.** Wipes only the slack space for each file and leaves the files themselves untouched (see Lesson 8, "Setting File Attributes," for a definition of slack).

Follow these steps to wipe files:

1. From the main Wipe Information screen, select the Files button. Wipe Information displays the Wipe Files dialog box as shown in Figure 14-3.

2. If you started Wipe Information from the Norton menu, you may need to change directories. Select the Directory button to display the Change Directory screen. Enter the new directory name or choose it from the list box. Select OK to return to the Wipe Files dialog box.

3. Enter the file specification in the File Name text area and select the other file name options as needed. Note that, for added safety, you can ask Wipe Information to confirm the wipe operation for each file.

4. Choose a wiping method.

5. Select the Wipe button. Wipe Information displays an attention box warning you that you are about to permanently wipe the selected files. Select the Wipe button to continue.

6. If you chose the Confirm each file option, Wipe Information displays a dialog box that shows the first file to be wiped. Your options are to Skip the file, Wipe the file, or turn off the confirmation feature (the Auto button). (You can also choose to Stop the wipe). Select the appropriate button.

7. The wipe continues, file by file, in the same fashion (unless you chose Auto to turn the confirmation off). When Wipe Information is finished, it displays a message box that tells you how many files were wiped. Select OK to return to the main Wipe Information screen.

File Name text area

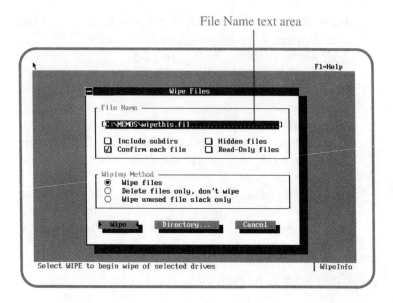

Figure 14-3. The Wipe Files dialog box.

Using Wipe Information to Permanently Wipe Drives

Two methods are available for wiping drives:

- **Wipe entire drive.** Wipes the system area and the data area according to the Wipe Configuration. If you are using the government wipe, you will have to reformat the disk if you want to use it again.

- **Wipe unused areas only.** Wipes files that have been deleted and other areas of the disk not currently in use. Note that this does not include the file slack areas. To wipe these areas, see the previous section.

Follow these steps to wipe a drive:

1. From the main Wipe Information screen, select the Drives button. Wipe Information displays the Wipe Drives dialog box.

2. Select the drive that you want to wipe (you can select more than one).

3. Select a wiping method.

4. Select the Wipe button to proceed with the wipe. Wipe Information displays an attention box warning you that you are about to permanently wipe the drive you selected.

5. Select the Wipe button to continue. Wipe Information displays a window showing you the progress of the wipe.

   Cancelling the Wipe You can cancel the wipe at any time by clicking on the Stop button or by pressing Enter. Wipe Information begins the wipe in an unused part of the disk, so the sooner you cancel the procedure, the better your chances are of saving your data.

6. A message box appears, telling you when the wipe is complete. Select OK to return to the main Wipe Information screen.

Quitting Wipe Information

To quit the Wipe Information program,

- From the main Wipe Information screen, select the Quit button or press Q.

99

Protecting Your System Against Viruses and Damage

In this lesson, you will learn how to use the Disk Monitor to protect your system against damage caused by computer viruses, ill-behaved software programs, and physical knocks.

Your Files Need Protection

Computer viruses are a nasty fact of life. A few of these programs are benign and merely annoying—they display cute messages or cause characters to "fall off" your screen. Most viruses, however, are downright vicious and have no other purpose in life but to trash your valuable data. Other software programs come armed with good intentions but, because of poor programming or system incompatibility, can end up running amok and destroying large chunks of your hard disk in the process. The Norton Utilities Disk Monitor program can help prevent these disk disasters from occurring.

What Disk Monitor Does

Disk Monitor is a memory-resident utility that watches the file activity on your system. It enables you to prevent other programs from accessing specified files without your permission. If a program attempts to gain access to a protected file, Disk Monitor alerts you and gives you the option of aborting the access or allowing it to continue. This way, your files are protected from viruses or runaway programs.

Disk Monitor also offers two other features: Disk Light and Disk Park. Disk Light displays, in the upper right corner of the screen, the name of any drive that is being accessed. This is handy if you have a drive light that is broken or if the drive is positioned where you cannot see it. As long as Drive Light displays the drive letter, you know not to turn off your computer or attempt to remove a disk from the drive. The Disk Park feature moves the read/write heads of your hard drive over data-free areas on your hard disk so that, if you move or bump the computer, the heads don't crash down on any tracks that contain data.

Read/Write Head This device travels back and forth across the surface of the disk to store information on the disk and retrieve information from the disk.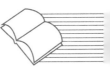

Running Disk Monitor

To start Disk Monitor, either select the **Disk Monitor** command from the Norton menu, or type **diskmon** at the DOS prompt and press Enter. The main Disk Monitor screen is displayed (see Figure 15-1).

101

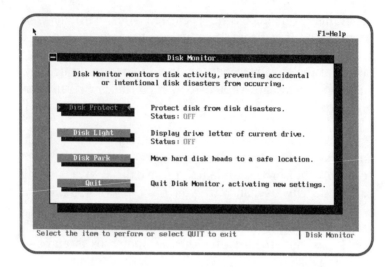

Figure 15-1. The main Disk Monitor screen.

Protecting Your Files with Disk Protect

The Disk Protect portion of Disk Monitor watches over your files and prevents other programs from accessing them without your permission. You can set four levels of protection:

- **System Areas** Prevents programs from writing to any part of the disk's system area or changing any system file.

- **Files** Prevents programs from changing any files that have the extensions you specify. Disk Monitor allows you to enter exceptions to this list. For example, you could specify that all files with a .COM extension should be protected. But some of these programs can modify themselves (with configuration information, for example). Through trial and error, you can identify these files and add them to the exceptions list.

- **System Areas and Files** Combines the two options above.

- **Entire Disk** Prevents programs from accessing any part of the disk. No files can be added, modified, or erased without your permission. Use this option only if you suspect that a virus exists on your system.

Whichever level of protection you choose, it applies to all the disks on your system. However, Disk Monitor does allow you to turn off Disk Protect for floppy disks. This is recommended, for example, if you are going to format a floppy disk.

If a program tries to access one of your specified files while Disk Protect is active, Disk Monitor will display a warning message. For example, if a program tries to modify a protected file, you will see the message

A write operation was attempted on a protected file. Do you wish to allow this operation?

You must then press Y to allow the access, N to disallow it, or D to disable protection.

Disabling Protection Because of the nature of Disk Monitor's protection, a single operation, such as formatting a floppy disk, may generate many protection messages. Temporarily disabling protection gets you through the operation much more quickly. Just be sure to turn the protection back on when the operation is complete.

Follow these steps to configure and run the Disk Protect feature of Disk Monitor:

103

1. From the main Disk Monitor screen, select the **Disk Protect** button. Disk Monitor displays the Disk Protect dialog box (see Figure 15-2).

2. Select a protection level.

3. If you chose either **Files** or **System Areas and Files**, you can also modify the Files and Exceptions list boxes. The Files list contains five default extensions that you can modify or delete as needed. You can also add your own extensions up to nine. The Exceptions files can be specific file names, or you can use wild cards to specify a group of files.

4. If you don't want to protect floppy disks, activate the **Allow Floppy Access** check box.

5. Select **ON** to activate Disk Protect. (Note: if Disk Protect is already running, you can deactivate it by selecting **OFF**.) Disk Monitor returns you to the main screen.

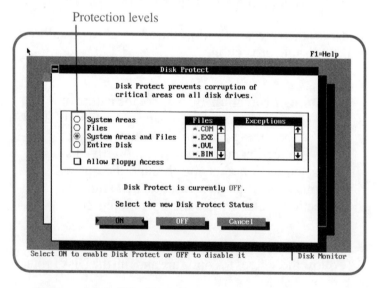

Figure 15-2. The Disk Protect dialog box.

Activating Disk Light

Follow these steps to run Disk Monitor's Disk Light feature:

1. From the main Disk Monitor screen, select the Disk Light button. Disk Monitor displays the Disk Light dialog box.

2. Select ON to activate Disk Light. (Note: if Disk Light is already running, you can deactivate it by selecting OFF.) Disk Monitor returns you to the main screen.

Running Disk Park

Follow these steps to run Disk Monitor's Disk Park feature:

1. From the main Disk Monitor screen, select the Disk Park button. Disk Monitor parks the hard disk read/write heads, sounds a beep, and displays the Disk Park dialog box (see Figure 15-3).

2. Turn off your computer with Disk Monitor still running to keep the drive heads parked. If you select Cancel or perform any other operation, Disk Monitor unparks the read/write heads and returns you to the main screen.

Quitting Disk Monitor

To exit the Disk Monitor program,

- From the main Disk Monitor screen, click on Quit, or press Q.

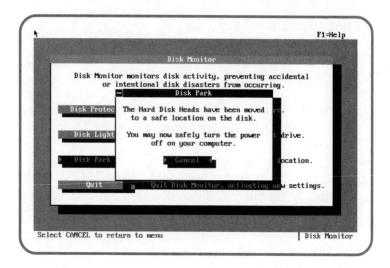

Figure 15-3. The Disk Park dialog box.

Loading Disk Monitor Automatically

You can get the most out of Disk Monitor if you have it running in memory all the time. Now that you have configured the Disk Protect feature, you can add Disk Monitor to your AUTOEXEC.BAT file so it loads automatically when you start your system. To have The Norton configuration program do this for you, perform the following steps:

1. Start NUCONFIG either by selecting **Configuration** from the main Norton program or by typing **nuconfig** at the DOS prompt and pressing Enter. The Norton Utilities Configuration dialog box appears.

2. Select the **AUTOEXEC.BAT** button. NUCONFIG displays the AUTOEXEC.BAT Setup dialog box.

3. Activate the Load the DISKMON Utility check box.

4. Select OK or press Enter. NUCONFIG displays the revised AUTOEXEC.BAT file.

5. Select the Save button to accept the changes. NUCONFIG returns you to the main Configuration screen.

6. Quit NUCONFIG by selecting the Quit button and selecting Yes in the dialog box that appears.

7. Reboot your computer to put the changes you made to your AUTOEXEC.BAT file into effect.

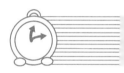

Protection Anytime You can run Disk Monitor's Disk Protect, Disk Light, and Disk Park functions from the DOS prompt. See your Norton Utilities User's Guide for more information.

In this lesson, you learned how to protect your files from viruses and runaway programs by using the Disk Monitor utility. In the next lesson, you will learn how to use the Norton Utilities Disk Tools program.

107

Lesson 16
Using Disk Tools

In this lesson, you will learn how to use the utilities contained in the Disk Tools program.

About Disk Tools

The Norton Utilities Disk Tools program is a collection of disk-related utilities that enable you to perform valuable disk protection and recovery operations.

Running Disk Tools

Follow these steps to run the Disk Tools program:

1. Start Disk Tools either by selecting Disk Tools from the Norton menu, or by typing disktool at the DOS prompt and pressing Enter. The Disk Tools introduction box appears.

2. Select Continue to display the Disk Tools menu (see Figure 16-1).

Select a Disk Tools Utility from the Procedures window...

...and information about it appears in the Description window

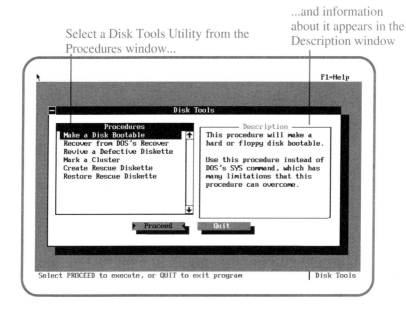

Figure 16-1. The Disk Tools menu.

The Disk Tools menu is divided into two parts. The Procedures window lists the six Disk Tools utilities, and the Description window displays a brief description of the highlighted utility.

Make a Disk Bootable

It is possible to bypass your hard disk at startup and boot from a floppy disk. This technique is used most often when the system area of a hard disk has been corrupted and can no longer boot itself. The Make a Disk Bootable option enables you to create a bootable floppy disk by copying the necessary system files onto the disk.

You can also use the Make a Disk Bootable option to copy fresh system files to a hard drive that is no longer bootable.

109

Follow these steps to make a bootable disk:

1. From the Disk Tools menu, highlight the **Make a Disk Bootable** option and select **Proceed**. Disk Tools displays a list of the disk drives in your system.

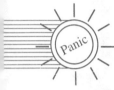

> **Bootable Floppy Drives** You can boot only from a floppy disk that is in drive A. Your computer's startup routine will ignore any other floppy disk even if it contains system files.

2. Choose a drive from the list and select **OK**. A message box appears asking you to insert a disk in the proper drive.

3. Insert the disk if you have not already done so, and select **OK** to continue. Disk Tools displays a window that tells you what is happening.

4. When Disk Tools has completed the procedure, a message box appears, telling you that the disk is now bootable. Select **OK** to return to the Disk Tools menu.

Recover from DOS's Recover

RECOVER is a DOS command that is supposed to restore all readable information from a disk with bad sectors. Unfortunately, RECOVER's restoration process makes a real mess out of the disks' contents. It moves all files and subdirectories to the disk's root directory and gives them cryptic names like FILE0001.REC, FILE0002.REC, etc. It also destroys the names of the files and directories in the old root directory. Sorting out the original file and directory names can take hours and is often impossible.

Norton Disk Doctor The Norton Disk Doctor program does a much better job of fixing disk errors than DOS's RECOVER command. See Lesson 17, "Diagnosing and Repairing Problems with Disk Doctor."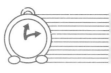

Disk Tools' *Recover from DOS's Recover* option restores the disk to its original state. Only the original root directory names cannot be recovered. To restore these names, you will have to use DOS's RENAME command and the Norton Change Directory program.

When To Recover from DOS's Recover You should use the *Recover from DOS's Recover* tool only if you have previously used the DOS RECOVER command on the disk, or if the disk's root directory has been destroyed.

Follow these steps to recover from DOS's Recover:

1. From the Disk Tools menu, highlight the **Recover from DOS's Recover** option and select **Proceed**. Disk Tools displays an introductory message explaining the uses of this option.

2. Select **OK** to continue. Disk Tools displays a list of disks to recover.

3. Choose a drive from the list and select **OK**. A message box appears asking you to insert a disk in the proper drive.

4. Insert the disk if you have not already done so, and select **OK** to continue. Disk Tools displays a message box that warns you to use this option only if you have previously used RECOVER, and asks if you are sure you want to continue.

111

5. Select **Yes**. Another message box appears to warn you that the files created by RECOVER will be lost.

6. Select **Yes** to start the recovery. Disk Tools displays a map of the disk area that you can use to monitor the progress of the recovery.

7. When Disk Tools has completed the procedure, a message box appears, telling you that the directories have been renamed DIR0000, DIR0001, etc. You can use the Norton Change Directory utility to examine and rename these directories. The root directory files have been renamed FILE0000, FILE0001, etc. You can use the DOS RENAME command to restore the names of these files. Select **OK** to return to the Disk Tools menu.

Revive a Defective Diskette

There are a number of ways that a floppy disk can become defective. The disk surface could get scratched; the disk could be exposed to heat or a magnetic field; or, often, a disk that has been used many times simply wears out. When this happens, DOS will report an error of the form

Bad sector reading drive A: Abort, Retry, Ignore, Fail?

The *Revive a Defective Diskette* tool rewrites the physical format of the disk to overcome these problems, but leaves the data on the disk intact.

Follow these steps to revive a defective disk:

1. From the Disk Tools menu, highlight the **Revive a Defective Diskette** option and select **Proceed**. Disk Tools displays a list of drives.

2. Choose a drive from the list and select OK. A message box appears asking you to insert a disk in the proper drive.

3. Insert the disk if you have not already done so, and select OK to continue. Disk Tools takes a few moments to analyze the disk and then displays a progress window.

4. When Disk Tools has completed the procedure, a message box appears, telling you that the disk is revived. Select OK to return to the Disk Tools menu.

Mark a Cluster

The *Mark a Cluster* tool enables you to mark any cluster on a disk as bad. This will tell DOS not to store any information in that cluster. You can also mark bad clusters as good, and DOS will then use those clusters to store files.

This tool is the manual version of a procedure that is done automatically by the Norton Disk Doctor utility. If you are having problems with a disk, I recommend that you let Disk Doctor do the work for you. See Lesson 17, "Diagnosing and Repairing Problems with Disk Doctor."

Create a Rescue Diskette

The *Create a Rescue Diskette* tool copies vital information about your hard disk to a floppy disk. It saves three types of information:

- **Partition Tables** A description of the physical setup of your hard disk.

113

- **Boot Records** The boot information for you system.

- **CMOS Values** Setup values used by some AT-compatible computers. These values are stored in a CMOS RAM chip inside the computer. This chip is powered by a small battery. If the battery is weak, the computer may have trouble finding disks, booting, or keeping the correct date and time.

Do not confuse a rescue diskette with a bootable diskette. If you cannot access your hard drive, the bootable diskette will only give you control of the operating system. The rescue diskette allows you to restore the information listed above to the hard drive.

To create a rescue disk, follow these steps:

1. From the Disk Tools menu, highlight the Create a Rescue Diskette option and select Proceed. Disk Tools displays the Create Rescue Diskette dialog box (see Figure 16-2).

2. Select OK to continue. Disk Tools displays a list of drives.

3. Insert a disk in the appropriate drive and choose the drive from the list.

4. Select OK. Disk Tools copies the rescue information to the disk.

5. A message box appears, telling you that Disk Tools has copied the rescue information successfully. Select OK to return to the Disk Tools menu.

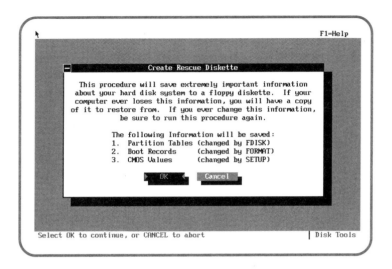

Figure 16-2. The Create Rescue Diskette dialog box.

Restore Rescue Diskette

If you are unable to access your hard disk and the Norton Disk Doctor cannot fix the problem (see Lesson 17, "Diagnosing and Repairing Problems with Disk Doctor"), you'll need to use the rescue diskette to restore some or all of the information contained on the disk. In many cases, you may need to restore only the CMOS values (when the battery dies). See Lesson 19, "Getting Information About Your System Hardware," to learn how to check the status of the CMOS battery.

To restore the information saved to the rescue disk, follow these steps:

1. From the Disk Tools menu, highlight the **Restore Rescue Diskette** option and select **Proceed**. Disk Tools

115

displays a warning message telling you that you should restore the rescue information only if you cannot access your hard drive.

2. Select **Yes** to continue. In the dialog box that appears, you can select the specific pieces of the rescue information you want restored: Partition Tables, Boot Records, or CMOS values.

3. Select the appropriate rescue data and then press **OK** to restore the information.

4. A message box appears, telling you that Disk Tools has restored the rescue information successfully. Select **OK** to return to the Disk Tools menu.

Quitting Disk Tools

To exit the Disk Tools program

- From the Disk Tools menu screen, select the **Quit** button.

Tools from the DOS Prompt You can skip the Disk Tools menu screen by running Disk Tools from the DOS prompt and adding switches to the disktool command. See your Norton Utilities User's Guide for information.

In this lesson, you learned how to use the Disk Tools utilities. In the next lesson, you will learn how to fix disk problems with the Norton Disk Doctor program.

Lesson 17
Diagnosing and Repairing Problems with Disk Doctor

In this lesson, you will learn how to diagnose and repair disk problems using the Norton Disk Doctor program.

Disk Problems

Previous lessons showed that there are many ways to lose valuable data. You can delete files or format disks accidentally, runaway programs can eat away at your hard disk, and viruses can trash your entire system. And, as if all this isn't enough, your disks can simply go bad. Information on the disk can become corrupted through poor workmanship or just general wear and tear. If the problem occurs in the disk's system area, the disk may become unreadable.

The Norton Utilities, once again, can help you recover from such problems. The Norton Disk Doctor program can diagnose what is wrong with your disk and, with your OK, repair the problem. You can also use Norton Disk Doctor as a form of preventive maintenance. By running the Norton diagnostics on a regular basis, you may catch disk problems early, before they do any serious damage.

The Disk Doctor Tests

The tests that Disk Doctor performs on your disks fall into two categories: the Diagnostic Tests and the Surface Test.

The Diagnostic Tests

The Diagnostic Tests check the integrity of the information stored in the system and data areas of your disk. Disk Doctor runs six different diagnostic tests:

- **Partition Table** Checks the hard drive partition.

- **Boot Record** Checks DOS startup information.

- **File Allocation Table** Checks directory and file allocation table.

- **Directory Structure** Checks each directory for readability and proper structure.

- **File Structure** Checks each file for readability and proper structure.

- **Lost Clusters** Checks for clusters that don't belong to any directory or file.

If Disk Doctor detects any disk problems during these tests, it will explain to you what the problem is and will ask if you want to fix it. If Disk Doctor makes any repairs, you have the option of creating an UNDO file that will allow Disk Doctor to restore a disk to its original condition should something go wrong.

Let Disk Doctor Make the Repairs You should always let Disk Doctor repair the problems it finds. It usually takes only a few seconds and you can always undo the changes later.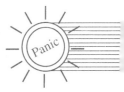

The Surface Test

The Surface Test scans your disk for physical defects. If Disk Doctor finds any disk errors, it will move the readable parts of the data to a good section of the disk and will mark the defective section as bad to prevent your computer from storing information there in the future. You can configure the Surface Test to make the test as exhaustive as you like using these parameters:

- **Test** You can choose between the slower Disk Test that scans every section of the disk, or the faster File Test that scans only disk areas that contain files.

- **Passes** You can tell Disk Doctor to make up to 999 passes of the disk surface. The default value is 1, which is a good setting for detecting most problems. However, some disk errors appear only intermittently. For these cases, you can either specify a multiple pass or have Disk Doctor test the disk continuously.

- **Test Type** You can choose between the *Daily test* that performs a quick scan of the disk, or the *Weekly test* that performs a comprehensive test on every disk sector. The Weekly option is two to three times slower than Daily. A third option, called *Auto Weekly*, is also available. Auto Weekly runs a Daily test every day except on Friday when it runs a Weekly test.

- **Repair Setting** You can choose how you want Disk Doctor to handle surface defects. You can specify that Disk Doctor not repair the disk, prompt you before repairing the disk, or repair the disk automatically.

Running Norton Disk Doctor

Start Disk Doctor either by selecting Disk Doctor from the Norton menu, or by typing ndd at the DOS prompt and pressing Enter. The main Disk Doctor screen appears.

Configuring the Surface Test

To configure the Disk Doctor Surface Test, take the following steps:

1. From the main Disk Doctor screen, select the Options button. Disk Doctor displays the Disk Doctor Options dialog box.

2. Select the Surface Test button. The Surface Test Options screen appears as in Figure 17-1.

3. Select the options you want and press OK to return to the Disk Doctor Options box.

4. Select Save Settings to store your selections. Disk Doctor returns you to the main screen.

Diagnosing a Disk

To diagnose a disk using Norton Disk Doctor, follow these steps:

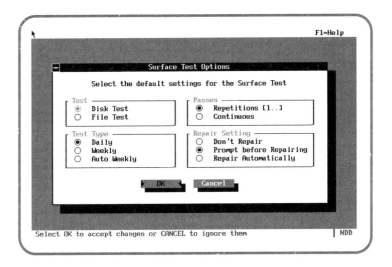

Figure 17-1. The Surface Test Options screen.

1. From the main Disk Doctor screen, select the **Diagnose Disk** button. Disk Doctor displays a list of the drives on your system.

2. Use the space bar to tag the drives you want Disk Doctor to test (you can choose more than one). A check mark appears beside each selected drive.

3. Select **Diagnose** to continue. If you chose a floppy disk, Disk Doctor prompts you to insert the disk in the drive. When you have done so, select **OK**.

4. Disk Doctor analyzes the disk and then proceeds through the six diagnostic tests.

5. If Disk Doctor detects any problems, it displays a message box like the one in Figure 17-2. Read the description of the problem carefully and then select **Yes** to have Disk Doctor make the necessary repairs. After

the first problem, Disk Doctor will ask if you want to create an UNDO file. Select **Yes** and enter the drive where you want the file saved.

6. When Disk Doctor completes the diagnostic tests, it displays the Surface Test screen showing the options you chose when you configured Surface Test. To use different options, you can change them at this time.

7. Select **Begin Test** to run the Surface Test (or you can select **Cancel** to skip the test). Disk Doctor displays a disk map enabling you to monitor the progress of the test.

8. When all tests are complete, Disk Doctor displays the Summary screen. Select **Report** to view the results of the tests.

9. You can choose to print the report by selecting the **Print** button, or you can save it to a file by selecting the **Save as** button. You can also simply view the file on the screen by selecting **Done** when you are finished. Disk Doctor returns you to the main screen.

Undoing Disk Doctor Repairs

Most of the time, Disk Doctor's repairs are successful and you will have no problems using the files on the disk. On rare occasions, however, a file may end up worse off than before it was "fixed." If you told Disk Doctor to create an UNDO file (you should always do this), you can easily restore the disk to its original condition by following these steps:

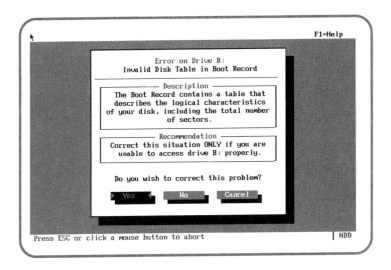

Figure 17-2. Disk Doctor has detected a problem.

1. From the main Disk Doctor screen, select the Undo Changes button. Disk Doctor prompts you to enter the drive where you saved the UNDO file.

2. Select the appropriate drive from the list. Disk Doctor searches for the file and, if it finds it, displays the date you saved the file and asks if you are sure you want to UNDO the changes.

3. Select Yes to continue. Disk Doctor restores the disk in just a few seconds and then displays a completion message.

4. Select OK to return to the main Disk Doctor screen.

Other Disk Doctor Options

Disk Doctor allows you to set two other options:

123

- Display a custom message to the user when a problem is found.

- Instruct Disk Doctor to skip certain tests.

Displaying a Custom Message

Use this option to prevent a user from making repairs to a disk. Disk Doctor displays your message but does not allow the user to make repairs. Follow these steps to display a custom message:

1. From the main Disk Doctor screen, select the Options button. Disk Doctor displays the Disk Doctor Options dialog box.

2. Select the Custom Message button. The Set Custom Message screen appears as shown in Figure 17-3.

3. Activate the Prompt with Custom Message check box.

4. Enter your message in the box provided.

5. Select OK to return to the Disk Doctor Options dialog box.

6. Save your changes by selecting the Save Settings button. Disk Doctor returns you to the main screen.

Skipping Certain Tests

Use this option if parts of your system are not fully IBM-compatible. Follow these steps:

Custom message

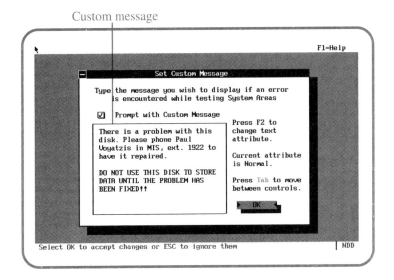

Figure 17-3. The Set Custom Message screen.

1. From the main Disk Doctor screen, select the **Options** button to display the Disk Doctor Options dialog box.

2. Select the **Tests to Skip** button. The Tests to Skip screen appears.

3. Choose the tests you want to skip.

4. Select **OK** to return to the Disk Doctor Options dialog box.

5. Save your changes by selecting the **Save Settings** button. Disk Doctor returns you to the main screen.

Quitting Disk Doctor

To exit the Disk Doctor program, from the main Disk Doctor screen, select the **Quit Disk Doctor** button or press Q.

Improving the Performance of Your Hard Disk

In this lesson, you will learn how to increase the efficiency of your hard disk using Speed Disk.

Understanding Speed Disk

When DOS stores a file on your hard disk, it looks for the first available cluster (see the "Determining File Size" section in Lesson 8 for a definition of cluster). If the file is too big to fit in a single cluster, DOS stores part of the file in the first cluster and tries to place more of the file in the next cluster. If the next cluster is already being used, DOS searches for the first free cluster. In this way, a file's contents end up being stored in several different places on the disk. Such a file is said to be *fragmented*.

As you add and delete files, your files become increasingly fragmented. This slows down your hard disk because a fragmented file takes longer to access than one that resides in *contiguous* (neighboring) clusters. The longer access time occurs because DOS must look in several different places for the complete file. If left unchecked, file fragmentation can slow even the fastest hard disk to a crawl.

Speed Disk optimizes your hard disk by physically rearranging the files so each file is stored in contiguous clusters.

Speed Disk Precautions Because Speed Disk reorganizes your hard disk, you should take some precautions before using it. First, remove from memory any memory-resident programs that may access the disk while Speed Disk is running. If you are not sure which programs to remove from memory, consider booting from a floppy disk to get a "plain-vanilla" DOS. Second, you should back up your hard disk. Speed Disk is unlikely to damage your system, but a power failure in the middle of a Speed Disk session would result in lost data.

Optimizing Your Hard Disk with Speed Disk

Follow these steps to run the Speed Disk program:

1. Start Speed Disk either by selecting Speed Disk from the Norton menu, or by typing speedisk at the DOS prompt and pressing Enter. Speed Disk performs a brief memory test to ensure that the data will not be corrupted during the operation, and prompts you for the drive you want to optimize.

2. Choose your hard drive from the list and then select OK to continue. Speed Disk analyzes your disk and then displays a message box showing the recommended optimization method (see Figure 18-1).

127

3. Select the **Optimize** button from the Recommendation window. Speed Disk begins the optimization process. The Status window displays the progress of the optimization. The Legend window explains the symbols used in the disk map.

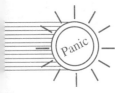

Interrupting Speed Disk While the Speed Disk optimization is in progress, do not turn off or reboot your computer. Doing so will seriously damage your files. If you must interrupt Speed Disk, press the Esc key, and Speed Disk will give you the option of cancelling or resuming the operation.

4. When Speed Disk finishes optimizing the disk, it sounds a beep and displays a completion message. Select **OK** to continue.

5. In the dialog box that appears, select **Exit Speed Disk** to return to DOS.

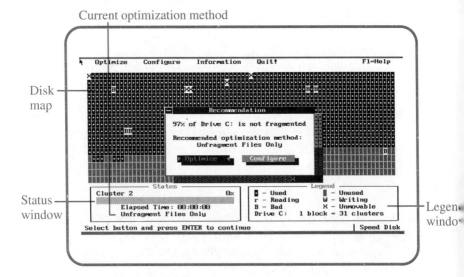

Figure 18-1. Speed Disk recommends an optimization method.

Using Other Optimization Methods

Speed Disk analyzes your hard disk and recommends an optimization procedure. The Speed Disk recommendation is usually the best method for your system. There are times, however, when you might want to use an optimization method that is more or less thorough. Here are the available optimization methods:

- **Full Optimization** Unfragments all files and moves the free space between files to the end of the disk. By moving free space to the end of the disk, Speed Disk allows files you subsequently save to be stored in contiguous clusters, reducing future fragmentation.

- **Full with DIR's First** Same as Full but also optimizes directory access.

- **Full with File Reorder** Same as Full but also optimizes directory and file access. This is the most complete method of optimization but takes the longest to run.

- **Unfragment Files Only** Unfragments as many files as possible, but does not move free space to the end of the disk. If your hard disk is nearly full, some large files may not get unfragmented. This is the fastest method.

- **Unfragment Free Space** Moves all data to the front of the disk but does not unfragment files. Use this method if you need to make room to copy a large file to your hard disk.

Which method should you use? For day-to-day use, Unfragment Files Only is sufficient. Run Speed Disk with this method about twice a week. Use Speed Disk with the Full Optimization method about once a month.

Selecting Different Optimization Methods

To run Speed Disk and choose an optimization method manually, follow these steps:

1. Start Speed Disk either by selecting Speed Disk from the Norton menu, or by entering speedisk at the DOS prompt. Speed Disk performs a brief memory test and prompts you for the drive you want to optimize.

2. Choose your hard drive from the list and then select OK to continue. Speed Disk displays the Recommendation window.

3. Select the Configure button from the Recommendation window. Speed Disk pulls down the Configure menu.

4. Press ← or click on Optimize to pull down the Optimize menu.

5. Select Optimization Method. Speed Disk displays the Select Optimization Method dialog box (see Figure 18-2).

6. Choose the optimization method you want to use and press OK. Speed Disk returns you to the Optimize menu. The method you selected appears in the Status window.

7. Select Begin optimization to execute the optimization process.

8. When Speed Disk is finished, a completion box appears. Select OK to continue.

9. To return to DOS, select **Exit Speed Disk** from the dialog box that appears.

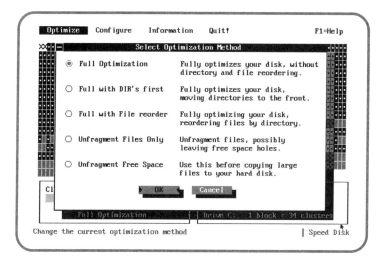

Figure 18-2. The Select Optimization Method dialog box.

In this lesson, you learned how to increase the performance of your hard disk using the Speed Disk program. In the next lesson, you will learn how to use the Norton Utilities to get information about your system's hardware.

Lesson 19
Getting Information About Your System Hardware

In this lesson, you will use the System Information program to learn about your system's hardware.

The System Information Utility

The System Information program enables you to examine all the facets of your computer. This includes everything from your system's hardware configuration to performance comparisons with other personal computers. If you are having problems with your computer, you can use System Information to get detailed data on your system's setup, memory usage, and disk characteristics. System Information can even print out a report on any aspect of your system.

In this lesson, you will use System Information to examine your hardware and memory configuration. In Lesson 20, you will learn how to get hard disk information and run performance tests.

Running the System Information Program

To start the System Information program, do the following:

1. Select **System Info** from the Norton menu, or type **sysinfo** at the DOS prompt and press Enter. The System Summary screen appears. (We will discuss this screen in the next section.)

2. Press Esc or select the System Summary **Cancel** button. System Information displays the System pull-down menu.

   The System Information program consists of six pull-down menus: System, Disks, Memory, Benchmarks, Report, and Quit!. The System Summary that is displayed when you start System Information is actually the first option from the System menu. In this lesson, we will discuss the System and Memory menus.

The System Menu

If the System menu is not displayed, click on **System** in the menu bar or use the arrow keys to activate it. The System menu contains six options that display detailed information about your hardware and software usage, as well as system, video, and network summaries.

The System Summary

The System Summary screen (see Figure 19-1) provides very general information about your computer system.

133

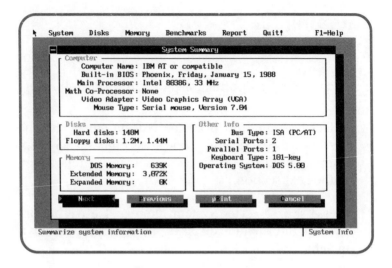

Figure 19-1. The System Summary screen.

To view the System Summary, do the following:

1. Select the **System summary** option from the System menu. The System Summary screen appears as in Figure 19-1.

2. Select **Cancel** or press Esc when you want to return to the System menu.

Moving Through the Options Use the **Next** and **Previous** buttons on each System Information screen to move sequentially through the menus. For example, selecting **Next** on the System Summary screen moves you to the Video Summary screen.

The Video Summary

The Video Summary screen displays detailed information about your system's video configuration. This includes your video adapter, monitor, and video memory. To view the Video Summary, select the Video summary option from the System menu. The Video Summary screen appears as shown in Figure 19-2. Press Esc when you want to return to the System menu.

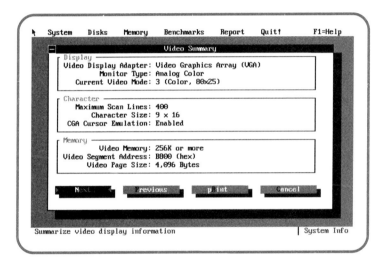

Figure 19-2. The Video Summary screen.

Hardware Interrupts

A *hardware interrupt* is a mechanism for hardware devices such as a keyboard or disk drive to request service from the processor. The processor, in turn, manages these interrupts to prevent communications from getting crossed. The Hardware Interrupts screen lists all the hardware interrupts that are set on your system. To display the listing of hardware

135

interrupts, select the Hardware interrupts option from the System menu. System Information displays the Hardware Interrupts screen. Press Esc when you want to return to the System menu.

Software Interrupts

A *software interrupt* is similar to a hardware interrupt except that a software program generates the interruption. The Software Interrupts screen lists all the software interrupts that are set on your system. The Owner column tells you the name of the last software program to use the interrupt. To display a listing of software interrupts, select the Software interrupts option from the System menu. System Information displays the Software Interrupts screen. Press Esc when you want to return to the System menu.

CMOS Values

The CMOS Values screen contains information on how your computer is configured. The values you see are stored in a CMOS RAM chip inside your computer (this feature is not available on XT-compatible computers). This chip is powered by a small battery. If you find that your computer begins to show improper dates and times, or has trouble finding your disks, it may be that the battery is weak. Check the CMOS Status box to see if System Information has discovered any problems with the battery. If there are any problems, consult your computer's operating manual. To view the CMOS values,

1. Select the CMOS values option from the System menu. System Information displays the CMOS Values screen.

2. Select Cancel or press Esc when you want to return to the System menu.

The Memory Menu

To pull down the Memory menu, click on Memory in the menu bar or use the arrow keys to activate it. The Memory menu contains six options that display detailed information about your system's memory usage.

The Memory Usage Summary

The Memory Usage Summary reports how your computer's RAM is being used. System Information divides the screen (see Figure 19-3) into three areas:

- **DOS Usage** Displays the amount of memory accessible to DOS. System Information reports how much of the total memory is being used by programs (and DOS itself) and how much is available to other programs.

- **Overall** Displays the total system memory. This includes the main memory (roughly equivalent to the total shown in the DOS Usage section), the display memory (memory used by video adapters), and the *expanded* and *extended* memory (these terms are defined later in this lesson).

- **BIOS Extensions** Lists the ROM (Read Only Memory) addresses for control programs on board cards, such as video adapters and disk controllers. The BIOS (Basic Input/Output System) uses these addresses to locate and execute the control programs each time you start your computer.

137

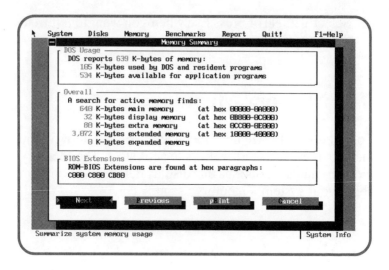

Figure 19-3. The Memory Summary screen.

To view the Memory Usage Summary, take the following steps:

1. Select the **memory Usage summary** option from the Memory menu. The Memory Summary screen appears as in Figure 19-3.

2. Select **Cancel** or press Esc when you want to return to the Memory menu.

Displaying Expanded Memory Usage

Expanded memory is add-on memory that certain programs (such as Lotus 1-2-3) can access to work with larger amounts of data. You must have an expanded memory board and a memory manager program present on your system to use this option. The Expanded Memory screen gives you detailed information on expanded memory usage in your system. To view the Expanded Memory screen,

1. Select the **Expanded memory (EMS)** option from the Memory menu. System Information tests your expanded memory and displays the Expanded Memory screen.

2. Select **Cancel** or press Esc when you want to return to the Memory menu.

Displaying Extended Memory Usage

Your computer's main memory is located inside chips installed on the computer's system board. Memory above 1 megabyte is called *extended memory*. You must have a 80286 or higher processor and an extended memory manager present on your system to use this option. The Extended Memory screen gives you detailed information on extended memory usage in your system. To view the Extended Memory screen, follow these steps:

1. Select the **exTended memory (XMS)** option from the Memory menu. System Information tests your extended memory and displays the Extended Memory screen.

2. Select **Cancel** or press Esc when you want to return to the Memory menu.

The Memory Block Listing

The Memory Block screen shows you how the memory available to DOS is being used. To view the Memory Block listing, select the **memory Block list** option from the Memory menu. The DOS Memory Blocks screen appears. Press Esc when you want to return to the Memory menu.

139

The TSR Programs Listing

A TSR (terminate-and-stay-resident) program is an application that remains active in memory when it is not in use. These programs are also called *memory-resident* programs. The TSR Programs screen displays a listing of all memory-resident programs currently occupying RAM. Use this listing to monitor the amount of RAM that your TSRs are consuming. To view a listing of TSR programs on your system, select the TSR programs option from the Memory menu. The TSR Programs screen appears. Press Esc when you want to return to the Memory menu.

The Device Drivers Listing

Device drivers are programs that enable DOS to interface with special hardware devices such as a mouse. The Device Drivers screen lists all drivers currently loaded on your system. To view the Device Drivers listing, select the Device drivers option from the Memory menu. System Information displays the Device Drivers screen. Press Esc when you want to return to the Memory menu.

In this lesson, you learned how to use the System Information utility to explore your system hardware. In the next lesson, you will use System Information again to get information about your hard disk and to run some performance tests.

Hard Disk Information and System Performance

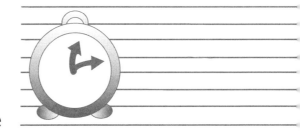

In this lesson, you will use the System Information utility to get information about your hard disk and to compare the performance of your system with that of other personal computers.

System Information Revisited

In the previous lesson, you learned how to use the Norton Utilities System Information program to get information about your computer's hardware and memory usage. System Information can also give you information about your computer's disks and can run benchmark tests to measure your system's performance.

Running these tests periodically can help alert you to system problems. For example, if you notice a marked decrease in your hard disk performance, you should consider running the Speed Disk utility (see Lesson 18, "Improving the Performance of Your Hard Disk").

Running the System Information Program

To start the System Information program,

1. Select **System Info** from the Norton menu, or type **sysinfo** at the DOS prompt and press Enter.

2. System Information displays the System Summary screen (you learned about this screen in the previous lesson). Press Esc to remove this screen and activate the pull-down menus.

The System Information program consists of six pull-down menus: System, Disks, Memory, Benchmarks, Report, and Quit!. In this lesson, we will discuss the Disks, Benchmarks, and Report menus.

The Disks Menu

To display the Disks menu, click on **Disks** in the menu bar or use the arrow keys to activate it. The Disks menu contains three options that display detailed information about your computer's disks: *Disk summary*, *disk Characteristics*, and *Partition Tables*.

The Disk Summary

The Disk Summary provides a list of the disks available on your system. For each disk, System Information displays the drive letter, the type of disk, the disk size, and the default (active) directory. To view the Disk Summary,

1. Select the **Disk summary** option from the Disks menu. System Information displays the Disk Summary screen.

2. To return to the Disks menu, select **Cancel** or press Esc.

The Disk Characteristics Screen

The Disk Characteristics screen gives you detailed statistics on all of your computer's disks. You can use this screen, for example, to determine the cluster size for you computer. This tells you how DOS stores your files and how much slack space is created by your smaller files. (*Cluster* and *slack* were defined in the "Determining File Size" section in Lesson 8). Simply multiply the Bytes per sector value times the Sectors per cluster value (see the example that follows). To display the Disk Characteristics screen, follow these steps:

1. Select the **disk Characteristics** option from the Disks menu. System Information displays the Disk Characteristics screen as shown in Figure 20-1. For my computer, the cluster size is 4,096 bytes (512 bytes per sector times 8 sectors per cluster).

2. You can use the list box on the right side of the screen to select a different drive.

3. To return to the Disks menu, select **Cancel** or press Esc.

The Partition Tables Listing

The Partition Tables list shows how your hard disk has been divided or *partitioned* into different hard drives. This information will tell you if your hard drive is partitioned

143

into *logical drives* and will indicate the size of each logical drive. To view the Partition Tables list, do the following:

1. Select the **Partition Tables** option from the Disks menu. System Information displays the Partition Tables screen.

2. To return to the Disks menu, select **Cancel** or press Esc.

Multiply these two values to find your system's cluster size

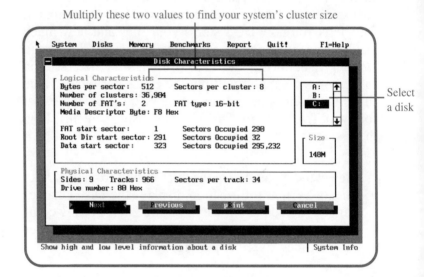

Figure 20-1. The Disk Characteristics screen.

The Benchmarks Menu

To display the Benchmarks menu, click on **Benchmarks** in the menu bar or use the arrow keys to activate it. The Benchmarks menu contains four options that measure the performance of your system. This lesson covers *CPU speed, Hard disk speed,* and *Overall Performance Index.*

Measuring CPU Speed

This test measures the performance of your computer's Central Processing Unit (CPU).

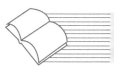

Central Processing Unit The CPU contains your computer's internal storage, processing, and control circuits. It runs your programs, processes your keyboard or mouse input, and controls the output that you see on a monitor or printer.

System Information displays the speed of your system relative to some other popular computers. Figure 20-2 shows the CPU Speed graph. System Information uses the IBM PC XT running at 4.77 MHz as the base of comparison. Compared to the XT's Computing Index of 1.0, the 8 MHz IBM AT rates a 4.4, while the 33MHz Compaq 386 clocks in at 34.7. You can interpret these numbers to mean that the AT is 4.4 times faster than the XT, while the Compaq is 34.7 times faster. The top bar shows the Computing Index of your computer. System Information runs the CPU test constantly, so the Index value may fluctuate if you move your mouse.

To run the CPU Speed test, follow these steps:

1. Select the CPU speed option from the Benchmarks menu. System Information displays the CPU Speed graph.

2. To return to the Benchmarks menu, select Cancel or press Esc.

145

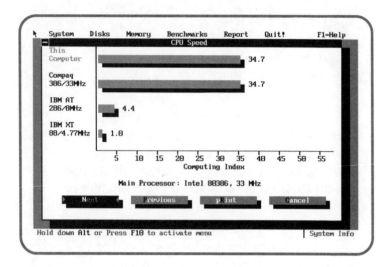

Figure 20-2. The CPU Speed graph.

Measuring Hard Disk Speed

This test measures the performance of your hard disk. As with the CPU Speed test, System Information compares your computer with the IBM XT, the IBM AT, and the Compaq 386. Figure 20-3 shows the Disk Speed graph.

The result shown for your system can be affected by the level of file fragmentation on your hard disk. (File fragmentation, and its remedy, were discussed in Lesson 18, "Improving the Performance of Your Hard Disk".) As an exercise, you should try running the Disk Speed test before you defragment your files. Make a note of the Disk Index (the graph value) as well as the seek times and data transfer rate listed below the graph. Then, retest your disk after you have optimized it with Speed Disk. You should see an improvement in all the numbers. To run the Hard Disk Speed test, do the following:

1. Select the Hard disk speed option from the Benchmarks menu. System Information displays the Disk
   Speed graph.

2. To return to the Benchmarks menu, select Cancel or
   press Esc.

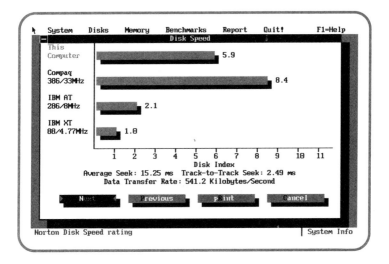

Figure 20-3. The Disk Speed graph.

The Overall Performance Index

This test combines the Computing Index and the Disk Index
to arrive at a composite performance index.

To calculate the Performance Index and display a
performance index graph,

1. Select the Overall Performance Index option from the
   Benchmarks menu. System Information displays the
   Overall Performance Index graph.

147

2. To return to the Benchmarks menu, select Cancel or press Esc.

The Report Menu

Pull down the Report menu. This menu contains three options that allow you to create reports of your system information: *view CONFIG.SYS*, *view AUTOEXEC.BAT*, and *Print report*.

Saving Reports As a precaution, you should keep a printout of each of these reports. The CONFIG.SYS and AUTOEXEC.BAT files contain important information used by DOS when you start your computer. If these files are accidentally deleted or modified, you can restore them using the printout. The comprehensive printout generated by the **Print report** option enables you to look for changes in your system that may be affecting performance.

The CONFIG.SYS File

This option enables you to view and print out the contents of your CONFIG.SYS file. Take the following steps:

1. Select the view CONFIG.SYS option from the Report menu. System Information displays the contents of your CONFIG.SYS file.

2. To print a copy of the file, select the pRint button.

3. To return to the Report menu, select Cancel or press Esc.

The AUTOEXEC.BAT File

This option enables you to view and print out the contents of your AUTOEXEC.BAT file. To do this, follow these steps:

1. Select the **view AUTOEXEC.BAT** option from the Report menu. System Information displays the contents of your AUTOEXEC.BAT file.

2. To print a copy of the file, select the **pRint** button.

3. To return to the Report menu, select **Cancel** or press Esc.

Printing a Report

You can use this option to get a printout of some or all of System Information's statistics. You can even include a report header and your own notes. Choose this option and respond to the dialog boxes to print a report of the four System Information categories: *System*, *Disk*, *Memory*, and *Benchmarks*. A fifth box allows you to choose *User Text* options.

In this lesson, you used System Information to get information about you hard disk and to test the performance of your system. You also learned how to generate a System Information report.

DOS Primer

This section explains the basics of DOS and some of the procedures you'll use when working with it.

DOS is your computer's Disk Operating System. It functions as a go-between program that lets the various components of your computer system talk with one another. Whenever you type anything using your keyboard, whenever you move your mouse, whenever you print a file, DOS interprets the commands and coordinates the task.

The following sections explain how to use DOS on your computer and what you can expect to see. I won't go into much detail, because now that you have The Norton Utilities, you won't need to know much about DOS.

Starting DOS

If you have a hard disk, DOS is probably already installed on the hard disk. When you turn on your computer, DOS automatically loads. If you don't have a hard disk, however, you must insert the startup disk that contains the DOS program files into the floppy disk drive before starting your computer. Respond to any on-screen prompts when DOS starts.

Changing Disk Drives

Once DOS is loaded, you should see a *prompt* (also known as the DOS prompt) on screen. It looks something like **A:>** or **A>** (or **C:>** or **B:>**) and tells you which disk drive is currently active. If you have a hard disk, the disk is usually labeled C. The floppy disk drives, the drives located on the front of your computer, are drives A and B. To activate a different drive,

1. Make sure there's a formatted disk in the drive you want to activate. (To learn about formatting, refer to Lesson 12, "Formatting Disks Using Safe Format.")

2. Type the letter of the drive followed by a colon. For example, type a:.

3. Press Enter. The DOS prompt changes to show that the drive you selected is now active.

Changing Directories

Because hard disks hold much more information than floppy disks, hard disks are usually divided into directories. For example, when you install The Norton Utilities, the Installation program suggests that you copy The Norton Utilities program files to a directory called *NU* on drive C. This directory then branches off from the *root directory* of drive C, keeping all the Norton Utilities program files separate from all the other files on drive C. Before you can work with the files in a directory, you must change to that directory. The following steps tell you how:

1. Change to the drive that contains the directory.

2. Type **cd***directory*, where *directory* is the name of the directory you want to access. (For example, type **cd\\nu**.)

3. Press Enter.

The backslash (\\) separates the names of the directories, giving DOS a *path* to follow in order to locate the directory at the end of the path. Use the backslash to separate all directories and subdirectories in a command line. A sample command line might look like this:

cd\\forests\\trees\\maples

Displaying a Directory Name If you change to a directory that you know exists and the directory name does not appear in the DOS prompt, type **prompt=pg** and press Enter.

Displaying a List of Files

To see a list of files stored in the current directory or on a floppy disk, use the DIR (Directory) command.

1. Change to the drive and directory whose contents you want to view.

2. Type **dir** and press Enter. A list of files appears.

If the list is too long to fit on the screen, it scrolls off the top. You can view the entire list by typing **dir/p** (pause) or **dir/w** (wide). If you type **dir/p**, DOS displays one screenful of files; you can see the next screen by pressing Enter. If you type **dir/w**, DOS displays the list across the screen, fitting many more file names on screen.

Copying Files

With DOS, you can copy a file from one drive or directory to another:

1. Change to the drive and directory that stores the file (or files) you want to copy.

2. Type the command line:

   copy *filename.ext* **d:***directory**filename.ext*

   where the first *filename.ext* is the name of the existing file you want to copy, *d:* is the drive to which you want to copy the file, and *directory* (optional) is a directory on the drive. The second *filename.ext* is the name you want to give the copy of the file; to use the same name, omit the second file name.

3. Press Enter. DOS copies the file and places the copy in the specified directory.

   Naming the Copied File If you copy the file to the same drive and directory, the two file names must differ. If you copy the file to a different drive or directory, the names can be the same or different.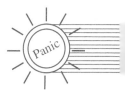

Deleting Files

To delete files using DOS, you use the DELETE (DEL) command, but be careful; if you delete a file by mistake, you may not be able to get it back:

1. Move to the directory that holds the file you want to delete.

2. Type the command line:

   del *filename.ext*

3. Press Enter. A message will appear, asking for your confirmation.

4. Type **Y** to delete the file or **N** to cancel the operation.

Accidently Erase a File? If you erase a file by accident, refer to Lesson 10, "Recovering Files with UnErase."

Renaming Files

Users often change their minds after naming a file. To change a file's name in DOS, use the RENAME (or REN) command:

1. Change to the drive and directory containing the file you want to rename.

2. Type the command line:

   ren *filename.ext filename.ext*

where the first *filename.ext* is the current name of the file, and the second *filename.ext* is the new name you want to assign to the file.

3. Press Enter. DOS renames the file and keeps it in the current directory.

Using DISKCOPY to Make Backup Copies of Program Disks

Before you install any program on your hard disk or run it from your floppy drive, you should make *backup copies* of the original program disks. By using backups to install or run the program, you avoid the risk of damaging the original disks.

Obtain a set of blank disks that match the original program disks in number, size, and density. For example, if your copy of The Norton Utilities came on four 3.5" 720K diskettes, obtain four 3.5" 720K (double-sided, double density) diskettes. The type of disk should be marked on the package. Because the DISKCOPY command copies the entire disk, you don't have to format the blank disks before you begin.

1. Change to the drive and directory that contains the DOS DISKCOPY file. For example, if the file is in C:\DOS, type **cd\dos** at the C:> prompt, and press Enter.

2. Type **diskcopy a: a:** or **diskcopy b: b:**, depending on which drive you're using to make the copies.

155

3. Press Enter. A message appears, telling you to insert the source diskette into the floppy drive.

4. Insert the original program disk you want to copy into the specified drive and press Enter. DOS copies as much of the disk into RAM as RAM can hold. A message appears telling you to insert the target diskette into the floppy drive.

5. Insert one of the blank disks into the floppy drive, and press Enter. DOS copies the information from RAM onto the blank disk.

6. Follow the on-screen prompts until DOS displays a message asking if you want to copy another disk.

7. Remove the disk from the drive, and label it to match the name of the original program disk.

8. If you need to copy another original disk, press Y and go back to step 4. Continue until you copy all the original disks.

9. When you're done copying disks, type N when asked if you want to copy another disk.

10. Put the original disks back in their box and store them in a safe place.

Is That All?

Now that you have The Norton Utilities, you don't need to know much more about DOS. You can use The Norton

Utilities to perform most of the operations normally accomplished in DOS, such as reorganizing your directories and locating files.

However, if you want more information about using DOS commands, see *The First Book of MS-DOS*.

Index

AUTOEXEC.BAT, 28
  viewing/printing contents, 149
  changing date and time stamp,
    55-56
  clusters, 57
CONFIG.SYS, 27
  viewing/printing contentf, 148
  copying, 153
  deleting, 154
  determining file's size, 57-58
  displaying
    erased files, 65
    list of, 152
  fragmented, 126-127
  IMAGE.DAT, 86
  printing, 59-62
  protecting with Disk Protect,
    102-103
  recovering deleted files, 63-69
  removing from disks
    permanently, 92-97
  renaming, 154
  searching for
    specified files, 40-43
    text within files, 47-49
  viewing, 45
floppy disks
  bootable, 109-110
  formatting, 78, 81-83
  reviving defective disks, 112-113
  saving hard disk information on,
    114-116
FORMAT command, 78
formatting floppy disks, 78
fragmented files, 126-127
full-screen mode, 6
function keys, 15

G–I

/G1 switch, 10
/G2 switch, 10
global switches, 9-10
/G0 switch, 10
hard disks
  measuring speed, 146
  saving information from/to
    floppy disks, 114-116
hardware interrupts, 135-136
/HEADERn switch, 60
help
  command line, 10
  context-sensitive, 20

/HERC switch, 10
/HID[+|–] switch, 54
hidden file attributes, 50
Home key, 16-17
Image program, 86, 90-91
IMAGE.DAT file, 86
initializing floppy disks, 78

K–L

keyboard
  navigating directories, 33
  selecting commands from pull-
    down menus, 14
keys for navigating dialog boxes, 16
/LCD switch, 10
Line Print program, 59-62
list boxes, 14, 17
  modifying for File Find, 44
  mouse actions, 19
/Ln /Rn switch, 61
logical drives, 144

M

make bootable diskette, 7
memory
  displaying usage, 139
  expanded, 137-138
  extended, 137-139
  reporting amount of RAM
    memory used, 137-138
memory-resident utilities, 100, 140
menus
  pull-down, 12
  selecting commands from,
    14-15, 18
MIRROR.COM utility, 87
modes
  command line, 6-8
  full-screen, 6
mouse
  actions used with dialog boxes,
    19
  navigating directories, 33
  selecting commands, 18
/MULTITASK switch, 10

N–O

/N switch, 61
/NOZOOM switch, 10
NUCONFIG program, 21
  expanding utilities, 29-30

160